GIDEON

The Mighty Man of Valor

**Bible Biography Series
Number Five**

John G. Butler

Copyright © 1992 by John G. Butler

Published by
LBC Publications
P.O. Box 3001
Clinton, Iowa 52732

Printed in the United States of America

ISBN 1-889773-05-0

*First printing 1992
Second printing 1995
Third printing 1998
Fourth printing 2001*

Introduction

The Bible Biography Series is a series of twenty books written about Bible characters by John G. Butler. These books are expository studies of the Scripture. They are extensively organized and outlined, filled with Gospel lessons and practical applications of Scripture to every day life, written in easy to understand laymen's language, and theologically and morally they take a strong, old-fashioned, fundamentalist position which is increasingly unpopular but greatly needed in our day.

These books are very helpful to preachers in providing material for sermons and lessons on these Bible characters and texts. They will also be found to provide much instruction for the individual in his or her personal Bible study; and because of their organized structure, they are very adaptable to Sunday School classes and Bible study groups.

The twenty books of the Bible Biography Series consist of books on *Joseph, Jonah, Elijah, Elisha, Gideon, Samson, John the Baptist, Peter, Abraham, Lot, Paul, Moses, Joshua, Samuel, David, Nehemiah, Jacob, Hezekiah, Mordecai,* and *Ruth*.

The author, a native of Iowa, is a long-time, fundamentalist, Baptist minister who has been teaching and preaching the Word of God for over forty-five years with nearly thirty-five years of pastoral experience. He pastored four churches, one each in Ohio, Michigan, Illinois, and Iowa. He is a veteran of the U.S. Navy, attended Tennessee Temple University and is a graduate of Cedarville University. He is also the author of the *Studies of the Savior,* a series of books about Jesus Christ.

Contents

    PREFACE..7

I. RUIN 9
    (Judges 6:1–10)
    A. The Explanation of the Ruin
    B. The Extent of the Ruin
    C. The Effect of the Ruin

II. REVELATION 22
    (Judges 6:11–24)
    A. The Care in the Revelation
    B. The Commission in the Revelation
    C. The Confirmation in the Revelation
    D. The Comfort in the Revelation

III. REFORMATION 40
    (Judges 6:25–32)
    A. The Orders for the Reformation
    B. The Obedience in the Reformation
    C. The Opposition to the Reformation

IV. RATIFICATION 55
    (Judges 6:33–40)
    A. The Fortifying of the Spirit Ratification
    B. The Following of the Soldiers' Ratification
    C. The Fleece of a Sheep Ratification

V. REDUCTION..71
    (Judges 7:1–8)
    A. The Purpose of the Reduction
    B. The Program for the Reduction
    C. The Promise in the Reduction

VI. REASSURANCE 84
    (Judges 7:9–15)
    A. The Proffer of Reassurance
    B. The Place of Reassurance
    C. The Product of Reassurance

VII. ROUT 97
    (Judges 7:16–22)
    A. The Strategy for the Rout
    B. The Specifics of the Rout

VIII. RANCOR 116
    (Judges 7:23 – 8:3)
    A. The Prelude to the Rancor
    B. The Protest from the Rancor
    C. The Placating of the Rancor

IX. RETRIBUTION 135
    (Judges 8:4–21,28)
    A. The Provoking of Retribution
    B. The Pursuit for Retribution
    C. The Punishment from Retribution

X. REQUESTS 156
    (Judges 8:22–27)
    A. The Dominion Request
    B. The Donation Request

XI. RELAPSE 173
    (Judges 8:28–35)
    A. The Conqueror's Relapse
    B. The Country's Relapse

    QUOTATION SOURCES 185

PREFACE

Gideon is a champion of the underdog. He was a nobody, yet he was called to lead the nation of Israel against its mighty foe, the Midianites. He stood virtually alone against the worship of Baal, yet he successfully tore down the altar of Baal and replaced it with an altar unto the Lord which was necessary if Israel was to have victory over the oppressing Midianites. He was limited by God to but 300 men, yet with that 300 he put to rout 135,000 Midianites and gave Israel one of its most miraculous victories ever. Thus, like David in his conquest of Goliath, Gideon is a great inspiration to all those who would endeavor to do great things for God in spite of tremendous disadvantages. His life teaches us that seemingly insurmountable difficulties can be successfully met head-on by anyone if they will only meet these difficulties by faith in God and His Word.

Gideon's great and inspiring work of delivering Israel from the Midianites was like a meteor racing across the sky—brilliant and spectacular indeed—but lasting only a few moments. We say this because, as few realize, Gideon's fame and his inclusion in Hebrews 11 in faith's Hall of Fame was a result of a performance which lasted only a few short days, maybe a week or so at the most. The rest of Gideon's life after the great victory over the Midianites is not elaborated on much in Scripture except enough to show its color—which is not glorious to behold but is morally slimy and spiritually degrading. And so while he is a great encouragement to the underdog, he is also a great warning to the victorious—a warning that continued victory over evil will not come unless we walk consistently by faith. We may have great accomplishments in the past, but those accomplishments will not secure victory for us in the future if we do not continue living by faith in God and His Word.

I.
Ruin

Judges 6:1–10

To properly study Gideon and his work of delivering Israel, we must begin our study by focusing on why Israel needed to be delivered. Joseph Parker rightly said, "We must realize this condition of things before we can understand the arduousness of the mission of Gideon. If we do not understand the situation we cannot understand Gideon's distress, hesitation, hopelessness."

Gideon came on the scene during the period of the Judges in Israel. This period of approximately four hundred years followed the settlement of Israel in Canaan under the leadership of Joshua and preceded the monarchy which began with King Saul. It was a dark period in Israel's history, so dark that J. Sidlow Baxter said, "Would that we might erase from the tablets of Israel's history the many dark doings and sad happenings which make up the bulk of this seventh book of the canon!" The last verse of the book of Judges sums up the darkness of those days by saying, "In those days there was no king in Israel; every man did that which was right in his own eyes" (Judges 21:25).

Thirteen of these Judges are recorded in the book of Judges. They include twelve men and one woman, and they come from eight different tribes of Israel. Gideon was the sixth Judge and one of the most prominent of the Judges. He and Samson, the thirteenth and last Judge in the book, have more recorded of them in the book of Judges than do any of the other Judges.

These Judges were raised up by the LORD to deliver the nation of Israel from great crisis. "The LORD raised up judges, who delivered them out of the hand of those who spoiled them" (Judges 2:16). When Gideon was thrust into his work of leading Israel, the Israelites were really being "spoiled" by the Midianites. In this study we will consider the awful ruin that characterized the land in Gideon's day, and from which Israel desperately needed deliverance. We will look at the explanation for the ruin, the extent of the ruin, and the effect of the ruin.

A. THE EXPLANATION FOR THE RUIN

"The children of Israel did evil in the sight of the LORD; and the LORD delivered them into the hand of Midian seven years . . . so it was, when Israel had sown, that the Midianites came up . . . . And they encamped against them, and destroyed the increase of the earth" (vv. 1,3,4). The explanation for why Israel was in such ruin was twofold. There was a primary and secondary cause. The primary cause was the iniquity of Israel; the secondary cause was the invasion by Midian.

1. The Iniquity of Israel

"Israel did evil in the sight of the LORD" (v. 1) was the primary reason for the ruin that plagued the Israelites. Sin always brings unnecessary suffering. Not so holiness. God gave commandments to bless us, not to burden us. "His commandments are not grievous [burdensome]" (I John 5:3). Sin, on the other hand, does not bless us but burdens us with untold grief. Therefore, as Matthew Henry said, "Let all that sin expect to suffer."

Both the particulars of Israel's sin and the perceiving of Israel's sin are spoken of in our text for this study.

The particulars of Israel's sin. "And I said unto you, I am the LORD your God; fear not the gods of the Amorites . . . but ye have not obeyed my voice" (v. 10). The specific sin mentioned in our text of which Israel was guilty was the sin of idolatry. As we will see in our next chapter, the particular idolatry they were guilty of was the worshiping of Baal. Worship affects how man walks; and so because of their worship of Baal, they would also be guilty of the gross immoralities—conduct that always accompanies idolatry. Good theology raises our morals, but bad theology lowers our morals. The low moral condition of our land evidences the corruption of the theology that prevails in our land.

The perceiving of Israel's sin. Note that Israel's evil was said to be done "in the sight of the LORD" (v. 1). Their sin was not hidden from God. No sin is. God is omniscient. He knows all about us. Psalm 139 underscores this fact: "Thou understandest my thought afar off . . . and art acquainted with all my ways. For there is not a word in my tongue, but, lo, O LORD, thou knowest it altogether" (Psalm 139:2–4). We may conceal our deeds and thoughts from man, but never will we conceal them from God. Therefore, we will have to reckon with God for all that we have ever thought, said, or done. A sobering thought indeed, and one that ought to clean up our lives.

2. The Invasion by Midian

The secondary cause of Israel's ruin was the invasion of the Midianites. But Israel, as we will see later, tried to make the secondary cause the primary cause. Mankind prefers to first put blame upon the Midianites of their lives as the main problem and to ignore their own doing of "evil in the sight of the LORD" as a factor. Interestingly, verse 1 puts "did evil in the sight of the LORD" first in the verse, and that is where it belongs, too, as the cause of Israel's ruin. Midian was the secondary cause. Midian was the rod of God's chastening hand, for it was "the LORD" who "delivered them [Israel] into the hand of Midian." When we are disciplined, it is not the chastening rod that is our primary problem, rather it is that which causes the use of the chastening rod. Samuel Ridout said, "The power of any enemy is put in his [the enemy's] hands by the unfaithfulness of God's people." It is not the enemy, but it is our unfaithfulness that causes the enemy to inflict us.

Looking at this secondary cause, we will note here the composition of the invaders, the corruption of the invaders, and the character of the invasion.

The composition of the invaders. The invaders were chiefly Midianites. But we learn from the Scriptures that the invaders also included some "Amalekites, and the children of the east" who came along with the Midianites and are mentioned three times (Judges 6:3,33; 7:12) in the story of Gideon as being part of this Midianite group. They came from east of the Jordan River, from the deserts to the east of Palestine. The Midianites were descendants of Abraham through his second wife Keturah (Genesis 25:1,2). The Amalekites were descendants of Esau (Genesis 36:12).

The corruption of the invaders. The Midianite record in Scripture will be forever stained by their unsavory conduct towards the Israelites during Moses' time. They, along with Moab, tried to get Balaam to curse the Israelites when they were being led by Moses toward Canaan. Failing in this they then resorted to corrupting the Israelites through their women (Numbers 23–25). Because of the evil the Midianites were to Israel, God commanded Moses to "Vex the Midianites, and smite them," and "Avenge the children of Israel of the Midianites" (Numbers 25:17; 31:2); and this Moses did and with decisiveness (Numbers 31:3–12). This decisive dealing with Midian was so effective that it was some two hundred years before Midian again became a problem for Israel.

What a good lesson this is on how to deal effectively with evil, a lesson we will see again in the story of Gideon. If we expect to conquer evil in our lives, we must oppose it with great earnestness. We must not give it any quarter, but must deal it strong and repeated blows.

While the Amalekites are a minor part of the Midianite invasion, it is worthy to note that they too have a record greatly stained with unsavory conduct. Specifically did they incur the curse of God when they attacked Israel shortly after Israel had escaped Egypt under Moses' leadership (Exodus 17:8–16). The attack by the Amalekites upon Israel was very cowardly, cruel, and crafty; for they "smote the hinder most of thee [rear of the camp], even all that were feeble behind thee, when thou wast faint and weary" (Deuteronomy 25:18). But Moses dealt firmly with them, too. He sent Joshua out to lead the Israelites in war against the Amalekites, and Joshua was most successful, for he "discomforted [overthrew] Amalek and his people with the edge of the sword" (Exodus 17:13). Later God said, "It shall be, when the LORD thy God hath given thee rest from all thine enemies round about, in the land which the LORD thy God giveth thee for an inheritance . . . thou shalt blot out the remembrance of Amalek from under heaven" (Deuteronomy 25:19). Israel was never to tolerate the Amalekites. Neither should we tolerate evil. All that Amalekites represents, we must forever oppose.

The character of the invasion. This was not primarily a military invasion like that of an army invading a land. True, the Midianites were armed (135,000 "drew sword" [Judges 8:10]) and could engage in military action; but they were more than an army. This invasion was more of a gypsy-type migration. Luke Wiseman said, "It was a general migration of the combined hordes of the desert; the same phenomenon, a thousand times magnified, as occurs summer after summer at the present day [1800s—the time of Wiseman's writing], when the roving Arabs of the Hauran and of Gilead come far up the plain of Esdraelon, plundering all they meet with." These hordes would come into the land during harvest time when they could plunder "the increase of the earth" (v. 4). Every year for "seven years" (v. 1) they "came up with their cattle and their tents" (v. 5) and "encamped against them [Israel]" (v. 4). It was no small group either, but a large host of people and animals that swarmed across the country. "They came as grasshoppers [locusts] for multitude; for both they and their camels were without number" (v. 5). The Midianites simply dominated the country. Israel no longer had dominion of their land.

Sin ever takes away dominion. "Israel had bowed to the gods of the heathen, therefore they must bow to the tyranny of the heathen" (Wiseman). And "If we act as the Israelites acted we shall suffer as they suffered" (Ibid.).

Gideon certainly had to deal with a formidable group in order to deliver Israel. It was comprised of some old and vicious enemies of Israel who had gained a great foothold in the land. Gideon's task was not going to be easy. But then it is never easy to take on evil when it is firmly entrenched in the land. Therefore it will take great dedication to fight the good fight against the foes of righteousness. A dedication that unfortunately we see very little of today.

B. THE EXTENT OF THE RUIN

The ruin of the land was great. For "seven years . . . Midian prevailed . . . and because of the Midianites, the children of Israel made themselves the dens which are in the mountains, and caves, and strongholds . . . And they [Midianites] encamped against them, and destroyed the increase of the earth . . . and left no sustenance for Israel . . . And Israel was greatly improvished" (vv. 1,2,4,6). As Matthew Henry did, we sum up the extent of the ruin of Israel in a twofold way: Israel was imprisoned and Israel was impoverished.

1. Israel was Imprisoned

"Because of the Midianites, the children of Israel made themselves the dens which are in the mountains, and caves, and strongholds" (v. 2). When the hordes of Midianites and their allies swarmed into Israel, the Israelites moved from the plains where their fields were and moved into the mountains to hide. Scripture cites three types of hiding places: dens (F. C. Cook says, "The word rendered 'dens' is only found in this passage. It is best explained of ravines hollowed out by torrents, which the Israelites made into hiding-places."), caves (Jamieson says some of the caves were capable of holding several thousand people), and strongholds (which are fortress like dwellings). Fearful of the Midianites, who not only plundered the crops but sometimes also murdered their victims (cp. Judges 8:18), they became virtual prisoners of the marauders by moving into these hiding places.

This hiding, justified as it may seem, was, however, cowardly action. It evidenced that Israel did not have the character to put up much resistance to this evil invading of the land by the Midianites. When the Midianites came into the land, the Israelites simply ran and hid. Wiseman said, "They had the character of too often preferring a dishonorable peace to an honorable though difficult resistance." Matthew Henry spoke likewise when he said, "This [hiding] was owing purely to their own timorousness and faint-heartedness, that they would rather fly than fight; it was the effect of a guilty conscience, which made them tremble at the shaking of a leaf . . . the heart that departs from God is lost, not only to that which is good, but to that which is great. Sin dispirits men, and makes them sneak into dens and caves."

Israel's actions are mirrored by many in our own land today—such as those who protest any war. Under the guise of being for peace, they oppose any armed conflict with others no matter what the issue. They are shortsighted in their reasoning, for they never seem to realize that there are times when it is better to shed some blood now rather than much more blood later. They are the kind who condemn the United States for dropping the A-bomb on Japan because of all the casualties it produced, but who will not admit that the A-bomb stopped the war and prevented much more casualties than it produced. It is the attitude that wants peace at any price, forgetting that peace of that kind is not peace at all.

But regardless of how clever these pacifists talk, we need to be reminded that it is generally corruption in character that produces such an attitude. Unwillingness to deal firmly with evil is a result of lack of character. It was Israel's problem, and it is also a problem in our society today. It even shows up in our churches, too, in their refusing to stand up against the dissident in the church. But such conduct is not charity; it is corruption!

2. Israel was Impoverished

The Midianites "destroyed the increase of the earth, till thou come unto Gaza, and left no sustenance for Israel, neither sheep, nor ox, nor ass . . . And Israel was greatly impoverished" (vv. 4, 6). Not only did the Midianites take the fruit of the crops, but they also took the Israelites' livestock. It was a wholesale plundering of the land that left the land in ruin materially. It was an economic disaster. Israel, however, was only reaping what they had sown. There was considerable justice in their experience. They had, because of their idolatry, failed to honor God with their substances. What they should have been giving God they gave to Baal. Now the Midianites take it all.

Israel had the same trouble in the time of the prophet Hosea. Hosea says, "She [Israel] did not know that I [God] gave her corn, and wine, and oil, and multiplied her silver and gold, which they prepared for Baal [instead of for Jehovah]. Therefore will I return, and take away my corn in its time, and my wine in its season, and will recover my wool and my flax given to cover her nakedness" (Hosea 2:8,9). Israel experienced God's blessings, but they used the blessings for the wrong things. Instead of honoring God with the blessings, they honored Baal; and that cost them dearly.

This problem continues today. God blesses us in many areas; but instead of using these blessings to honor Him, we use them to depart from Him. God gives us such things as health, wealth, convenience, and time which should enable us to really give much of ourselves to serving the Lord faithfully. But instead of service, about all God gets are excuses. People with all sorts of advantages complain they just are not able to serve regularly in the church. Such an attitude begs for judgment from God in the form of a stripping of their blessings. Hence, when we lose some of our blessings, we need to take serious thought as to whether we were using these blessings for God as we ought. Such serious thinking will prevent the loss of further blessings, for it will cause us to correct our delinquency and to be better stewards of what we still have left.

C. THE EFFECT OF THE RUIN

"And the children of Israel cried unto the LORD. And it came to pass, when the children of Israel cried unto the LORD because of the Midianites, That the LORD sent a prophet unto the children of Israel" (vv. 6–8). The troubles of Israel were salutary. They resulted in Israel coming back to God. How often this is the case. Trouble drives us to God. But as F.B. Meyer said, "Alas! that God has so often to drive men to Himself." Would that we responded better to God's chidings, so we did not have to always be brought low and put in painful circumstances before we finally turned to God.

The effect the ruin had upon the Israelites, as seen from our text, can be detailed in a twofold way. It produced prayer and it produced preaching.

1. The Praying It Produced

"And the children of Israel cried unto the LORD" (v. 6). The troubles with the Midianites caused Israel to pray to God. Their prayer was delinquent, diligent, and deficient.

A delinquent prayer. "When the children of Israel cried unto the LORD . . . the LORD sent a prophet" (vv. 7, 8). The "when" should have been a lot sooner than it was. For "seven years" (v. 1) they watched as the Midianites stripped their land bare at harvest time and stole their livestock. Finally they got around to praying to the Lord. But why did they wait so long before they sought God in prayer? The answer is that when we are far from God, we are not inclined to do much praying. When we are walking in disobedience to Him, we have little interest in praying even though our troubles are many. Prayer and disobedience do not go together. An example of this is seen in who the crowd is that attends the church's prayer meetings. The backslidden crowd is seldom there. They are not very interested in the prayer services. They may show up when a church service is entertaining, that is, when it has some musical or some celebrity featured; but they will not show much enthusiasm for the prayer service.

How often is it that the people who have the most problems are the least likely to pray. You can observe this in church again and again. You would think these folk who have so many problems in their lives would be the first ones to show up for prayer. But, no, they are generally the last to pray, the last to show up at the church's prayer service. This is one of the great perils of disobedience. Disobedience creates problems and puts within us disinterest in going where the problems can be solved.

A diligent prayer. Israel "cried" unto the Lord. The basic meaning of the word "cried" is to "cry out with a loud voice" (William Wilson). So there was great effort put forth in this prayer. They were earnest in their praying. They were not going through the motions. They were not mumbling through some prayer book in a monotone voice. They were in great distress because of the ruin which covered the land, and, therefore, they "cried" out for relief.

Earnestness is needed if our praying is to be acceptable. How can we expect God to get earnest about something we are praying about if we are not earnest about it? God is not in the business of paying much respect to prayers that lack earnestness. If we are not earnest in our request, we need not expect God to be earnest in His response.

A deficient prayer. The prayer was deficient because of the priority of its concerns. Some may wonder why it was deficient praying here to pray for deliverance from the Midianites, for Israel surely needed deliverance from the Midianites. The answer is that Israel first needed to be delivered from that which permitted the Midianites to come into their land. As we noted earlier, the problem of the Midianites was the secondary cause, not the primary cause. The primary cause was Israel's sin. But they were not praying about that. To correct this deficiency, to encourage them to continue to seek Him for help, and to begin to answer their prayer, God sent them a prophet who did some great preaching. We will consider this preaching next.

2. The Preaching It Produced

"When the children of Israel cried unto the LORD because of the Midianites . . . the LORD sent a prophet unto the children of Israel, who said unto them, Thus saith the LORD God of Israel, I brought you up from Egypt, and brought you forth out of the house of bondage; And I delivered you out of the hand of the Egyptians, and out of the hand of all who oppressed you, and drove them out from before you, and gave you their land; And I said unto you, I am the LORD your God; fear not the gods of the Amorites, in whose land ye dwell; but ye have not obeyed my voice" (vv. 7–10). The prophet God sent to Israel had a good message. This message, though especially needed by Israel in Gideon's day, gives us some important ingredients that need to be in every preacher's message in any age. This message can be divided into three parts: rescue, responsibility, and rebellion.

Rescue. The message reminded Israel that God had rescued Israel from great troubles in the past. "I delivered you out of the hand of the Egyptians, and out of the hand of all who oppressed you" (v. 9). Such a reminder would rebuke Israel for not seeking God sooner. But it would also encourage Israel that God was able to deliver them from the Midianites, too, and that they were therefore wise to come to Him for help, for He—not the idols they had been worshipping—was the One Who could help them. Our messages need to remind people of the greatness of God, and what He has already done for us.

Responsibility. The message reminded Israel of their responsibility to not go after other gods. God had plainly commanded them to not "fear [worship or serve] the gods of the Amorites, in whose land ye dwell" (v. 10). It is only fitting that they should be loyal to the God Who had delivered them from their enemies. We have an obligation to be faithful to God for what He has done for us. Any attitude to the contrary is grossly ungrateful and totally illogical.

One of our great problems today is the lack of emphasis on our responsibilities, on our obeying God's commands. We seem mostly concerned about what we want God to do for us, but not very concerned about what He tells us to do for Him. This problem includes our human relationships, too. We are more concerned about what others are doing for us than what we are doing for them. People will sign petitions, picket, and protest for their rights; but when it comes to their responsibilities, they seem to look only for excuses for not fulfilling them. Our messages need to put more emphasis on our obligations. Our messages not only need to tell of the promises of God, but also of the precepts of God.

Rebellion. The message rebuked Israel for their rebellion. The command to not go after other gods was disobeyed. "But ye have not obeyed my voice," (v. 10). This was the climax of the message from the prophet dealing with the deficiency in their prayer. It told Israel what their main trouble was, where they most needed help, and, therefore, what they really ought to be praying about first. Israel had been primarily concerned about the consequences of their evil, but God was primarily concerned about the cause of their evil. Israel was most concerned about their distress, but God was most concerned about their disobedience which brought about their distress. Israel was chiefly concerned about their material problems, but God was chiefly concerned about their spiritual problems which were the root cause of their material problems.

How wise it was for God to first deliver Israel from the problem of their sins before He delivered them from the problem of their suffering. It would have been a mistake to deliver Israel from Midian without first dealing with their spiritual problem, for if the cause of the problem is not dealt with then

Israel will not be given genuine help. So a prophet who indicts the people for their sin must precede a Gideon who delivers the people from their suffering. Before the people can be delivered from the evil of their circumstances, they must first become convicted about the evil of their conduct. This is always God's way. Therefore, John the Baptist must first come and proclaim to the people the sinfulness of their deeds before Jesus the Savior comes on the scene. Jesus must first come to save His people from the tyranny of their sins before He saves them from the tyranny of Rome. We must preach the holiness of God before the redemption of God will be properly appreciated and received. We must first be burdened with the guilt of our sin before we will be truly concerned about forsaking our sin. And a church asking God for help should not be surprised if He sends them a preacher who knows how to preach against sin.

The world, of course, does not like this order. The people in Jesus' day were more concerned about the tyranny of Rome than the tyranny of sin. Governments lay out billions for welfare without dealing with what causes welfare—alcohol, immorality, and just plain laziness. Churches preach a social Gospel trying to take people out of the slums without addressing the need of first taking the slums out of the people which produced the slums of their circumstances. Rescue Missions become more interested in addressing the material needs of their clients than in addressing their moral and spiritual needs. But such an approach will never work in solving men's problems because it does not get to the root cause of the problem. However, few seem to understand or are willing to accept this truth today—which explains why we are not doing a very good job in solving the problems of humanity, though we have tons of experts and programs highly praised by man.

With the preaching of the prophet, the stage is now set for Gideon to come on the scene to deliver Israel. Hearts have been prepared for him to do his work. The days of Midianite dominion are fast coming to an end.

II.

REVELATION

JUDGES 6:11–24

BEFORE GIDEON COULD become Israel's deliverer, he had to first come to know God in a very real, personal, and reverent way. To bring this about, God revealed Himself in a special way to Gideon. He came to Gideon in the form of "the angel of the LORD," the Old Testament revelation of the second person of the Trinity which some other notable Old Testament characters also saw in their experience. Hagar was visited by Him in the wilderness by a fountain of water when she had fled from Sarah (Genesis 16:7–13); Moses saw Him in the burning bush (Exodus 3:2); Balaam saw Him on the road of disobedience after his donkey saw Him first (Numbers 22:25,31); and Samson's parents also saw Him when He announced to them the coming of Samson (Judges 13:3–22). This Old Testament theophany was the turning point in Gideon's life. It transformed him from a man filled with doubts and unbelief, cowering before the Midianites, to the "mighty man of valor" (v. 12) which God called him when He first came to Gideon. This revelation was the prime mover for Gideon's work of delivering Israel.

One of the important keys to serving God is to know God well and to have a right relationship with Him. There must be a closeness to God, an understanding about God, and an awe of God if service is to be performed faithfully and gallantly. Our relationship with God cannot be distant, cold, or vague if we are going to serve with integrity, stand courageously against the mighty foes of God's people, know clearly God's orders, and be faithful in obeying God in spite of the difficulties of our circumstances. Today, we have so much emphasis on methods and programs for doing God's work, that we seem to forget that the most important thing for accomplishing great things for God is to be right with God. No method or program, as attractive and impressive as they may be to natural reasoning, will be of much help if we do not have a close personal relationship with the Lord. So before we plot and plan, before we organize and deputize, and before we enlist helpers and engage the enemy, we must come to know and bow down to God and His Word. Lacking these things, we will only beat the air instead of assault the adversary; for only "the people that do know their God shall be strong, and do exploits" (Daniel 11:32).

We will note the care (vv. 11–13), commission (vv. 14,15), confirmation (vv. 16–22), and comfort (vv. 22–24) in this great revelation given by God to Gideon.

A. THE CARE IN THE REVELATION

"And the angel of the LORD appeared unto him [Gideon], and said unto him, The LORD is with thee, thou mighty man of valor. And Gideon said unto him, O my Lord, if the LORD be with us, why then is all this befallen us? And where are all his miracles which our fathers told us of, saying, Did not the LORD bring us up from Egypt? But now the LORD hath forsaken us, and delivered us into the hands of the Midianites" (vv. 12,13). The first thing Gideon was informed about in this revelation was that God cared. But the *proclamation of God's care*, "The LORD is with thee," was met with a *protest about God's care*, "If the LORD be with us, why then is all this befallen us . . . ?" God said He cared; Gideon disagreed and said He did not. Let us examine the two claims.

1. The Proclamation of God's Care

When God said, "I am with thee," He spoke volumes concerning His care for His people. To be with His people means to be for His people, to be concerned for His people, and to provide for His people—in short to care for His people. God's current care for His people had been evidenced plainly in His having heard their cry of distress and in His having sent a prophet to prepare their heart for deliverance (6:8–10), which we noted in our last chapter. Furthermore, His coming to Gideon in his distress evidenced considerable care, too. Gideon's situation when this Divine revelation occurred certainly mirrored the conditions of Israel at that time because of the Midianite problem. The angel of the LORD found Gideon threshing wheat "by the winepress, to hide it from the Midianites" (v. 11). In a secluded out-of-the-way spot, Gideon was trying to thresh out some grain which the Midianites would not be able to plunder. Things were very bad in Israel, but God cared, and so He came to Gideon to reveal Himself and His deliverance to Gideon.

The great evidence of God's care for us is God's presence with us. We can survive the worst of circumstances if the Lord is with us; for His care will see us through the circumstances. This was demonstrated so well earlier in the Scripture in the case of Joseph (for further study of Joseph see author's book on Joseph). Sold into slavery in Egypt, he served in Potiphar's house. But "the LORD was with Joseph" (Genesis 39:2), and Joseph not only survived, but he even prospered (Ibid.). Circumstances soured later for Joseph because of the slander of Potiphar's wife, and Joseph was thrown into prison. But "the LORD was with him" (Genesis 39:23) there, too; and God's plan and purpose for his life was not thwarted but only advanced by these circumstances. When the Lord is with us, we need not fear His lack of care for us. When He is with us, no circumstance can overcome us even though that circumstance may appear outwardly to be our destruction.

2. The Protest about God's Care

It is very hard for the natural man to believe that God is with him and that God cares for him when providence has frowned long and hard upon him. It is very hard to believe that you possess great spiritual blessings ("the LORD is with thee" is indeed a choice spiritual blessing) when materially you are doing very poorly. This was Gideon's situation; and so walking by sight rather than by faith, he lashed out at God as many do in such situations. He said, "If the LORD be with us, why then is all this befallen us? And where are all his miracles which our fathers told us of, saying, Did not the LORD bring us up from Egypt? But now the LORD hath forsaken us, and delivered us into the hands of the Midianites" (v. 13). In that protesting statement, Gideon protested in a threefold way the idea that God cares. He protested about the justice of God, the power of God, and the faithfulness of God. It was not a nice statement. But his charges against God are made frequently by unbelief in every age. However, nothing he said was justified as we will see in examining these charges.

The justice of God. "Why then is all this befallen us?" This question blames God for Israel's troubles. It accuses God of being unjust in His treatment of Israel. It asks God in an accusative way why He is letting all these troubles come upon them. It is an age-old question asked by folk when troubles mount. It is a question that ignores the real cause of the problem and prefers to cast blame on God. But Gideon was wrong for making such a statement, for Israel "did evil in the sight of the LORD" (6:1), and that was the main cause of their problems. Gideon could not plead ignorance of the evil in the land either; for idolatry prevailed in Israel. His own father, in fact, had an altar of Baal right in his own home. But like many, Gideon shut his eyes to the real and obvious cause which was right before his own eyes and blamed God instead.

We will never solve our troubles until we look in the mirror and come to grips with the real cause of our troubles. Blaming God will never bring solutions. It is never God's fault. It is not His lack of care that is the cause of our problems. The reason "why" is always sitting on our own doorstep. But men still blame God for the evils of the land. We envy and hate; then blame God for fightings and wars. We live immorally, and then wonder where God is when we are plagued with terrible venereal diseases. We are greedy and violent; then when crime fills the land, we wonder where the God of love is. But the problem is not God's inadequacy; the problem is man's iniquity.

The power of God. "Where are all his miracles which our fathers told us of, saying, Did not the LORD bring us up from Egypt?" Gideon's next protest concerns God's power. Because the Midianites were oppressing Israel, Gideon concluded God lacked power to provide deliverance and to perform miracles. If God is with them, as the heavenly Guest insists, then Gideon concludes God must not have the power He used to have.

Gideon's problem in this particular protest was mistaking God's will for God's power, a common mistake we all make inexcusably often. If God is not willing, we then conclude God is not able. We are slow to allow God the right to exercise His power according to His purpose. And we are exceedingly slow to recognize that our sins often stop His willingness to help us. Isaiah said, "Behold the LORD's hand is not shortened, that it cannot save; neither his ear heavy, that is cannot hear. But your iniquities have separated between you and your God" (Isaiah 59:1,2). The prophet Hanani spoke along the same line when he said to King Asa, "The eyes of the LORD run to and fro throughout the whole earth, to show himself strong in the behalf of them whose heart is perfect toward him" (II Chronicles 16:9). It is not God's power that is deficient here; it is man's impurity.

The faithfulness of God. "The LORD hath forsaken us" was Gideon's last protest about God's care. But he had it all mixed up. God had not forsaken Israel, rather Israel had forsaken God. God was not unfaithful, but Israel was unfaithful. Israel had gone after Baal. But unbelief ever blames God for doing what it in itself has been doing. We fail; but rather than acknowledge our guilt, we accuse God of doing the sin. How strange and perverted does the mind of unbelief work! Sometimes we see this at church. Church grumblers, as an example, complain that the church does not care about them; but the truth of the matter is they do not care about the church. The sin they accuse the church of is the very sin they themselves commit abundantly.

Gideon's protest about God's care did not reveal any faults in God, nor did it nullify the claim that God was with His people and thus cared greatly for them. His protest only showed that Gideon had a long ways to go in his relationship with God before he was going to be Israel's deliverer. It showed why God had to work in Gideon's heart first before Gideon could be Israel's deliverer. Before Gideon delivers his people, he himself must be made right with God.

So it ever is with God's servants. We cannot serve well at all if we are not right with God ourselves. We must have our own heart cleansed, our own faith inspired and strengthened, and our own life true to God before we can be of service to God and help other people to be delivered from the oppressors of their soul. God, therefore, always starts first with His servants and cleanses and purifies their heart before He sends them into the vineyard to lead others to righteousness.

B. THE COMMISSION IN THE REVELATION

"The LORD looked upon him, and said, Go in this thy might, and thou shalt save Israel from the hand of the Midianites. Have not I sent thee?" (v. 14). God's answer to Gideon's protest about God's care was to commission Gideon to deliver Israel from the Midianite oppression. This deliverance from the Midianites would silence all his protest about God not caring.

We will note the person for the commission, the particulars of the commission, and protest about the commission.

1. The Person for the Commission

Gideon, in human reasoning, was not a likely candidate for the job of delivering Israel. When he first comes on the scene in Scripture, he is cynical of God's care and filled with doubts and unbelief. Furthermore, his station in life was not impressive either. He was only an obscure farmer who lived in a small insignificant town of Ophrah located in the tribal territory of

GIDEON

Manasseh (according to Jamieson, Ophrah is located about sixteen miles north of Jericho). He, like the rest of the Israelites, was busy hiding things from the Midianites.

But in spite of his unpretentious situation, Gideon was called "thou mighty man of valor" (v. 12). This was probably as much a revelation and surprise to Gideon as it was to everyone else. There was nothing in Gideon's life to indicate to the natural eye that he was a "mighty man of valor." In fact, the statement seems so inappropriate for Gideon at the time that J. Sidlow Baxter tries to make Scripture say the "mighty man of valor" phrase referred not to Gideon, but to the Lord. Baxter wants Scripture to say, "The LORD is with thee, even the LORD mighty in valor." We can understand Baxter's feelings because at that time Gideon had not demonstrated any discernible valor. But as esteemed a Bible teacher as Baxter is, his changing of Scripture is totally unwarranted. It was indeed Gideon who is described as a "mighty man of valor." God sees not as man sees. God looks on the heart, while man looks on the outward appearance (I Samuel 16:7). "Mighty man of valor" was obviously something known only to God at the time. Gideon himself did not equate the description as fitting him. But God does not make mistakes; and Gideon will indeed prove that God was right; for he will, after God gets through preparing him for his work, shortly demonstrate that he is "a mighty man of valor."

God calls a lot of folk into service who may not at the time of the initial call evidence much promise that they will be God's gallant servants. But it is not the man in himself that makes a gallant worker for God; it is what God can make that man which is the key to service. Let any person simply submit to God's plan and purpose for their life, as Gideon finally did, and God will make them what they need to be in order to do His work. "The first condition of spiritual strength and success is to give our hearts to God in profound loyalty" (J. T. Hamly). Therefore, do not despair that your small inventory of attributes will eliminate you from His service. Simply yield yourselves completely to the Lord, and He will make you able to serve Him.

We need to note here that one important reason God often calls those into His service who, like Gideon, appear deficient is that He, not the servant, will get credit for the work. Because of his lowliness, people would see that it was not Gideon but it was God Who worked through Gideon. That is exactly what God wants. The focus needs to be on God and His glory, not on man's greatness. "God hath chosen the foolish things of the world to confound the wise; and God hath chosen the weak things of the world to confound the things which are mighty; And base things of the world, and things which are despised, hath God chosen, yea, and things which are not, to bring to nought things that are, That no flesh should glory in his presence" (I Corinthians 1:27–29).

2. The Particulars of the Commission

The particulars of Gideon's commission involves basic principles found in every call to service given by God. We note four details of Gideon's commission which have universal application to those who serve God: the personalness of the commission, the priority of the commission, the power for the commission, and the promises with the commission.

The personalness of the commission. "The LORD looked upon him and said, Go . . . ." Here is Gideon's selection. The "looked at him" pointed out Gideon. It personalized the commission. It made sure Gideon knew God was speaking to him when He said, "Go."

God's calls are personal calls. He will speak to you personally, and you will know He is talking to you. Many, however, ignore this important principle in one's calling and so get mixed up and on the wrong track because they think they have a "Go" when they have never had the "looked upon him." They confuse the calls of others with their own call. While the big problem today is men refusing to go when they have been called to go, yet we must not overlook the fact that there is also the problem of some who think they are called who have not been called at all. Sometimes it is the emotion of the hour or even pride that causes some to think they have been told to "Go" when they never had the "looked upon him." However, you must be chosen before you are given a commission. Woe is he who gets in a calling that is not his. It is just as bad to try to be a Gideon when not called as to not go when called. Before we "go" we must make sure we have had the personal "looked upon him."

The priority of the commission. Two things dictated that this commission be given top priority in Gideon's life: the character of the commission and the communicator of the commission.

The first thing about the commission that dictated priority was the *character of it*. It was a command. "Go" is a command, not a suggestion or one of a dozen options for Gideon's life. Those who would serve must recognize their call as more than a solicitation. It is a command—hence, it demands great priority.

The second thing about the commission that dictated priority was the *communicator of it*. God Almighty communicated the call. "Have not I [the LORD] sent thee?" There is no higher authority than God. Lest anyone question that "the angel of the LORD" was indeed God, this verse clears it up with certainty. For when the angel of the Lord is speaking, we read, "the LORD . . . said, Go . . . Have not I sent thee?" Our verse makes it clear that Jehovah ("LORD") Himself is "the angel of the LORD" and is the One giving the commission to Gideon. Therefore, this commission must have first priority in his life. The rank of the one giving the commands dictates the priority of the commands. There is no higher rank than "the LORD"; therefore, this commission must have top priority in Gideon's life.

Few want to give this kind of priority to their service, however. Other interests and pursuits in life are often given higher priority. But if Gideon is to deliver Israel, he must make this the main emphasis of his life. Everything must focus on this work; he must give his all to it. Those who fail to fulfill their calling often fail because they did not give their calling the priority it should have. The world and carnal Christians will criticize top priority dedication to one's calling. But when the One giving the command holds the highest rank of all, we had better not pay any attention to the critics if we intend to serve acceptably.

The power for the commission. God told Gideon, "Go in this thy might." This might is not Gideon's own might, but the strength which God gave him, "i.e. the strength which thou [Gideon] hast, since Jehovah is with thee . . . The demonstrative 'this' points to the strength which had just been given to him through the promise of God [to be with him]" (Keil).

Thankfully we do not have to serve God in our own strength which is woefully inadequate for doing God's work. Though weak, yet we can say as Paul, "I can do all things through Christ, who strengtheneth me" (Philippians 4:13). Through the power of God the weakest of the weak can become the strongest of the strong.

The promises with the commission. Gideon received three most encouraging promises with his commission. While God may test our faith at times by giving us orders without accompanying promises, we will not serve long before we are acquainted with many uplifting promises as Gideon was.

The three promises were first, "Thou shalt save Israel from the hand of the Midianites" (v. 14); second, "thou shalt smite the Midianites as one man" (v. 16); and third, "I will be with thee" (Ibid.). The first two promises had to do with the success of his mission; the third promise had to do with the presence of God. The flesh will be more interested in the prospects of victory than in the presence of God, but we need to be more interested in having the presence of God with us. Moses was given similar promises in the wilderness (one that promised the presence of God and one that promised success) when God said to him, "My presence shall go with thee, and I will give thee rest" (Exodus 33:14). Moses quickly demonstrated which promise was more important when he said, "If thy presence go not with me, carry us not up from here" (Exodus 33:15). He said nothing about the promise of rest. He saw the presence of God as the best blessing of all, and he obviously and wisely felt that if he had that blessing then everything would be all right.

Our attitude should be the same. We should thank God for the promises of smiting the Midianites, of rest, and of success that may come. But the promise that should encourage us the most is the promise of His presence. When Christ gave the great commission, the clincher was "Lo, I am with you always, even unto the end of the world" (Matthew 28:20). Few things so encourage one in service for God as to know the presence of God will abide with him.

3. The Protest About the Commission

Again Gideon protested. He had previously protested God's care, now he protests God's commission. When God commissioned him he said, "O my Lord, wherewith shall I save Israel? Behold, my family is poor in Manasseh, and I am the least in my father's house" (v. 15). Gideon, like Moses years before, protests his call to be Israel's deliverer. Gideon's two excuses for objecting to his call were his lack of fortune and of fame. "My family is poor" and "I am the least in my father's house."

He lacked fortune. He was short on money—"my family is poor." But Israel's problem was not something money could solve. Not as many problems as we think can be solved by money. In fact, if your problems can be solved by money, you really do not have very big problems. If you are facing a big debt you may not appreciate that truth, but think it through before you reject it. Think of all the great problems that money cannot solve. Money really is not a great problem solver. Our government, of course, has not learned this truth yet and probably never will. But the Word reminds us periodically that money is not the answer. Gideon could not have solved Israel's problem with money. He needed more than money. He needed God—and God had promised to be with him. So lack of money was not a valid protest about his commission.

He lacked fame. Gideon said he was "the least in my father's house." Gideon's statement says he was the low man in the company. He had little status, rank, and position. He was not a V.I.P. He was an unknown, a nobody. But as Joseph Parker said, "We need not be socially great to be spiritually useful."

This truth is another hard one to learn. Even our churches do not demonstrate acceptance of this truth very well. This fact is seen in the emphasis some of our churches put on celebrity Christianity. When trying to get people to come to church, they often advertise that some famous person will be present to say (or sing) a good word for Jesus. But such advertising and parading of celebrities is nothing but a fleshly promotional gimmick and really does nothing for the cause of Christ. We do not need famous people in order to have a good Sunday and to experience great spiritual blessings in the services. We need men of faith, not men of fame. Gideon could be a man of faith, and he did become a man of faith (as is attested by his inclusion in faith's Hall of Fame in Hebrews 11). Fame was not essential, but faith was.

Gideon's emphasis in this protest was "not of what God was, but what he was; not what God could do, but what he, Gideon, might do" (Haldeman). When we look at things that way, we will always come to the same conclusion Gideon did. Without God we are worthless, useless, weak, and unable. "Except the LORD build the house, they labor in vain that build it" (Psalm 127:1). But God is building this house of deliverance for Israel, so Gideon has no legitimacy in his protest.

C. THE CONFIRMATION IN THE REVELATION

God's responses to Gideon's protests did not fall on deaf ears. The revelation of God given Gideon was beginning to get through to Gideon. Unbelief was fading. Faith was growing. The longer Gideon talked with his Visitor the more he began to suspect he was talking with some important heavenly creature. Finally, Gideon decided he wanted to confirm this fact; and so he said, "If now I have found grace in thy sight, then show me a sign that thou talkest with me" (v. 17). We will note the matter of confirmation and the means of confirmation.

1. The Matter of Confirmation

Gideon's request for a sign was not, as some think, evidence of unbelief—something most sign-asking generally is. This request did not manifest doubt in what God had just said. The request was not "show me a sign that what you say is true," but rather "show me a sign that thou talkest to me." There is a vast difference between the two requests. The former manifests unbelief. But the latter does nothing of the sort. The latter seeks to make sure the experience is real, not imaginative; that the source of the message is indeed Divine, not spurious.

Gideon is no longer protesting. He is no longer arguing with what has been said. He now simply wants to confirm the source of what he has heard. Is it indeed some heavenly authority that has been speaking to him, or is he daydreaming? Is this a true Divine message or not? As another said, "He sought a sign to satisfy himself that he was in a waking state, that his senses were not deceiving him, that the angel was not a mere phantom called up by a heated imagination" (G. A. Rogers).

The principle behind this request for confirmation that "thou talkest with me" is the principle stated by the Apostle John when he said, "Try the spirits whether they are of God; because many false prophets are gone out into the world (I John 4:1). For the health of our faith we need to verify truth and expose error. The devil delights in confusing our minds; so we do not distinguish between God speaking and someone else speaking, including our own imagination. He loves to deceive us into believing that what he says is from God, and what God says is unreliable or only a figment of our imagination or an irrational emanation of a sick mind. He often sends out his ministers to masquerade as "apostles of Christ" and "ministers of righteousness (II Corinthians 11:13,15) to try and beguile us into thinking that what they say is what God is saying. He will discredit true ministers of God by proclaiming that they are demon possessed and "mad; why hear ye him?" (said of Christ in John 10:20), "thou art beside [same word translated 'mad' at end of quote] thyself; much learning doth made thee mad" (said of Paul in Acts 26:24). So we need to examine the source of what we hear. Who is doing the speaking? Is the message Divine or is it diabolic? Honest examination is not skepticism, but it will help keep us from skepticism.

2. The Means of Confirmation

That which Gideon would use to examine and thus confirm the source of what he had just heard was to bring to his Guest a "present" which consisted of "a kid, and unleavened cakes of an ephah of flour" (v. 19). Gideon brought the "flesh . . . in a basket, and he put the broth in a pot, and brought it out unto him under the oak, and presented it" (Ibid.). The way in which his Guest would receive the gift would indicate whether Gideon had heard from a heavenly guest or from someone else posing as a Divine being or even from his own imagination.

Gideon learned quickly that his Guest was God. When Gideon brought the present to his Guest, He said to Gideon, "Take the flesh and unleavened cakes, and lay them upon this rock, and pour out the broth. And he did so. Then the angel of the LORD put forth the end of the staff that was in his hand, and touched the flesh and the unleavened cakes; and there rose up fire out of the rock, and consumed the flesh and the unleavened cakes. Then the angel of the LORD departed out of his sight" (vv. 20, 21). The heavenly guest made the present into an offering which was consumed by fire. An Israelite would quickly recognize God in such action, for they knew the fire on the altar spoke of God. Thus Gideon knew it was God. He "perceived that he was an angel of the LORD" (v. 22), which was tantamount to saying it was God Whom he had seen. The way in which the "present" was received confirmed it was God speaking. He knew it was not his imagination for now the "present" was nothing but ashes. Also he knew it was not an impostor, for only God could do with the "present" what happened to it.

Gideon did two things here that we all in principle can do which will lead to the confirmation of our faith. First, he sacrificed to the Lord, and second, he submitted to the Lord. His sacrifice was his "present." The "present" was indeed a sacrifice, especially when one considers the times in which he lived. His submission was evidenced by his following faithfully the commands of the Lord as to what to do with the "present." Shortly after this sacrifice and submission, he had all the confirmation he needed. Jesus said, "If any man will do his [God's] will, he shall know of the doctrine, whether it be of God, or whether I speak of myself' (John 7:17). Confirmation is never obtained by stingy (non-sacrificing), disobedient (unsubmissive) souls. Assurance and discernment comes to those who are devoted to the Lord. "He who gives himself to God, laying the devotion of his whole soul upon Christ . . . will find assurance that God talketh with him" (Henry T. Edwards). If doubts arise in your heart concerning God and His Word, the best way to prove your doubts wrong is to sacrifice and submit to God. God does not leave the devoted soul long in the dark about vital truths which that soul needs to know.

D. THE COMFORT IN THE REVELATION

"When Gideon perceived that he [the Visitor] was an [the] angel of the LORD, Gideon said, Alas, O Lord GOD! For I have seen an [the] angel of the LORD face to face. And the LORD said unto him, Peace be unto thee; fear not: thou shalt not die. Then Gideon built an altar there unto the LORD, and called it Jehovah-shalom" (vv. 22–24). The final work of the revelation given Gideon was to bring him great comfort. When it was confirmed that Gideon's visitor was indeed God, it caused great fear in Gideon's heart. "Alas, O Lord GOD! For I have seen an [the] angel of the LORD face to face." He feared death. "It was the received opinion among the Jews that any vision of the Divine glory would be fatal, in consequence of what God had declared to Moses. When Moses said unto the Lord, 'I beseech Thee show me Thy glory' the Lord said unto him, 'Thou canst not see

My face; for there shall no man see Me and live.'" (F. Elwin). Gideon, like Samson's parents later, felt he was doomed because he had seen God. Obviously a man in that state of mind does not have peace at all. But God met Gideon's need by giving him peace. What comfort that was for Gideon. No comfort is so great as God's peace. We note from our text the announcement of peace and the altar of peace.

1. The Announcement of Peace

No sooner had Gideon expressed his fears, and hence his lack of peace, than God said to him, "Peace be unto thee; fear not: thou shalt not die." Through the Word of God, Gideon learned of great peace; and Gideon found this peace with God in the only way man will ever find peace with God, namely, through Jesus Christ. The Angel of Jehovah, whom we believe is indeed the second person of the Trinity, was the One Who gave him this peace. Christ is the only One Who can give true peace to man and protect man from death before God. No man could stand in the presence of a thrice holy God and have peace were it not for Jesus Christ. It is Christ Who said, "Peace I leave with you, my peace I give unto you; not as the world giveth, give I unto you. Let not your heart be troubled, neither let it be afraid" (John 14:27). Paul ardently proclaimed this truth in his epistles, too. Examples include: "We have peace with God through our Lord Jesus Christ" (Romans 5:1), and "He is our peace" (Ephesians 2:14).

Yes, Gideon's experience is a wonderful illustration of the peace which the Gospel proclaims. When Christ was born the angels gave the same message, "Fear not . . . peace" (Luke 2:10,14), to the shepherds that "the angel of Jehovah" gave to Gideon. Elwin does a good job summing up the Gospel lesson from this experience of Gideon when he says, "How did Gideon live? The answer will open to us some precious gospel truths. Gideon saw the glory of God, indeed, but it was 'in the face of Jesus Christ.' 'No man,' says St. John, 'hath seen God at any time. The only begotten Son, who is in the bosom of Father, He hath declared him.' In other words, whenever there has been a manifestation of Jehovah to His creatures, it has been by Jesus Christ, the second person in the ever-blessed Trinity;' and it is by His having tabernacled in our flesh that the awful majesty of Jehovah has been softened into mildness and peace and love."

2. The Altar of Peace

This great event in Gideon's life demanded a memorial, so he built an altar and named it fittingly "Jehovah-shalom." This name combination means "the LORD our peace." The first word in the name, Jehovah (which is generally translated LORD or GOD in all capital letters), is the personal name of God. "The meaning of the word is Redeemer [which makes it such a fitting name for the second person of the Trinity]. Every time it is used in the Scriptures it is connected with deliverance by God" (Mark Cambron). The second word in the name, "Shalom," means peace. So when we connect these two words together we get "the LORD our peace."

Gideon's altar evidenced that he had come a long ways spiritually since His heavenly Guest came to visit him. It showed three important aspects of his growing faith: the wisdom, worship, and witness of his faith.

The wisdom of his faith. Gideon's altar indicated he had learned from this revelation where the source of peace was. He had learned that it was Jehovah Who could bring peace to man. We have so much learning in our world today, but few have learned this truth. Men have tried and continue to try a myriad of solutions for peace which leave out Christ. But they have never found true peace without Him. If Gideon is going to have personal peace and if he is going to bring peace to the land of Israel, he must know the source of peace. The altar says he does. Having this wisdom was an important qualification for his becoming the deliverer for Israel.

The worship of his faith. An altar speaks of worship. True faith worships. Gideon will worship Jehovah. Worship is essential if he is going to serve the Lord as Israel's deliverer. Jesus said, when solicited by Satan to worship him, "Thou shalt worship the Lord, thy God, and him only shalt thou serve" (Matthew 4:10). Thus He tied worship and service together.

You will serve whom you worship. Those who do not worship well do not serve well. People who are not regular in worship at church should not be put in places of service at church for they will not serve well. Gideon will serve well, however, for he indicated by his altar that he will worship Jehovah.

The witness of his faith. The altar was also a witness of Gideon's faith. And it was a very courageous witness, for he built this altar right in the vicinity of his father's altar to Baal. He has come to the place where his dedication to serving God is beginning to reflect the "mighty man of valor" title. He is not afraid to stand up and declare his loyalty to Jehovah even though all those around him are for Baal. Such a man will oppose evil gallantly.

Like Gideon, we live in a pagan world. All around us are the ungodly. If we are going to take any kind of stand for God it will have to be done before a hostile world. One will not do much testifying of his faith if he is unwilling to take his stand for God in the midst of a heathen world. If you limit your witness to a sympathetic crowd, you will have very little opportunity to stand for truth and righteousness, for even our churches are filled with many who oppose any strong stand for God.

We are now beginning to see clearly why Gideon will be Israel's deliverer. We may not have seen much in Gideon to justify his commission when we first saw him. But now we see much that justifies calling him a "mighty man of valor." And as we continue to read and study about him in the Scripture, we will see more and more why that title fits him well.

III.

REFORMATION

JUDGES 6:25–32

GIDEON HEARD FROM the Lord a second time. As Matthew Henry said, "God's visits, if gratefully received, shall be graciously repeated. Bid God welcome, and he will come again." Gideon had given honor to the first revelation from God by bringing a "present" (6:18) to the angel of the Lord and making a memorial altar to honor the Lord. Now God speaks to Gideon again.

The Lord did not wait long to speak to Gideon a second time. It occurred on the night of the day in which the Lord had first appeared to him. The subject of this second message to Gideon was about a religious reformation. Gideon was to stage a religious reformation in his father's home where he lived. "Reformation must precede deliverance. Gideon did not undertake the work of fighting the Midianites until he had first effected a religious reformation among his own people" (W. F. Adeney).

From the passage of Scripture before us, we will note the orders for the reformation (vv. 25,26), the obedience in the reformation (v. 27), and the opposition to the reformation (vv. 28–32).

A. THE ORDERS FOR THE REFORMATION

"The LORD said unto him, Take thy father's young bullock, even the second bullock of seven years old, and throw down the altar of Baal that thy father hath, and cut down the grove that is by it; And build an altar unto the LORD thy God upon the top of this rock, in the ordered place, and take the second bullock, and offer a burnt sacrifice with the wood of the grove which thou shalt cut down" (vv. 25, 26). These orders would test Gideon's commitment to God's service. Regarding this situation, F. B. Meyer said, "We are first tested in the less before being called to the greater." Before Gideon delivers a nation, he must first deliver a family. He must prove his commitment in the small task before he can be trusted with the large task.

From these two verses of our text we will consider the particulars of the orders, the purpose of the orders, and the place for the orders.

1. The Particulars of the Orders

These orders for the reformation were twofold. Gideon was to raze the altar of Baal and raise the altar of Jehovah.

Raze the altar of Baal. The worship of Baal had been widely accepted by the Israelites. Altars to Baal dotted the countryside. One of those altars belonged to Gideon's father. This was evidently more than just a personal altar, for "to judge from verses 28, 29 [it] was [also] the common altar of the whole family of Abiezer in Ophrah" (Keil). Right beside the altar of Baal stood the images (translated "grove" in our text in the KJV) which were related to the vile female goddess called Ashtaroth. She was considered the goddess of fertility and sometimes was even viewed as the progenitress of Baal. These images consisted of either poles or trees (hence the idea of groves) and were forbidden to be erected near the altar of Jehovah (Deuteronomy 16:21).

Gideon's orders instructed him to "throw down" the altar of Baal and to "cut down" the images of Ashtaroth which were beside the altar of Baal and which were associated with the worship of Baal. The orders, therefore, did not allow for any compromise with paganism. Gideon was to vigorously attack Baalism with sledgehammer force. He was to be unsparing in his action of opposing idolatry.

This is the only way to victoriously conquer evil as far as God is concerned. However, mankind seldom gets this enthused and earnest about eradicating sin from society and from their personal lives. In fact if one does get out the sledgehammer, he is duly reprimanded, told not to be a bull in a china closet, and exhorted to exercise more charity and compassion. We are so disgustingly sensitive about dealing with evil. As an example, the policeman can hardly make an arrest without some protester accusing him of "police brutality." Also in our churches, it has become nigh unto impossible to give adequate discipline for delinquent members. Members opposing discipline will cry "love" and "forgiveness" any time discipline is suggested. They forget or conveniently ignore that judgment is very vital and valid if holiness is to exist, and that without holiness we will not have real love and forgiveness. These members need to remember that the evil of Baalism had brought the terrible oppression of the Midianites upon Israel; and, therefore, it needed to be dealt with accordingly. We need to let the curse of sin guide us more when we take action against it. Too often in dealing with evil, we are guided by a sick, sentimental, soft-pedaling attitude of tolerance. But we must deal firmly with sin if we are to gain the victory over it. The altar of Baal must be razed. Do not leave a stone of that altar in place.

Raise the altar of Jehovah. The razing of the altar of Baal was to be followed by the raising of the altar of Jehovah. We note the essentialness, location, and the usage of the altar Gideon was to build.

First, the essentialness of the altar. Reformation required Gideon to do more than just tear down a false altar; he must also build a true altar. Reformation is not only destruction, but it is also construction. It is not only negative, but it is also positive. It is not enough to denounce sin; we must also preach righteousness. We must declare the anathema of Mount Sinai, but we must not stop there, for that is an incomplete work. We must complete the work by declaring the blessing of Calvary. W. F.

REFORMATION

Adeney speaks likewise when he says, "Reformation is not complete without the successful establishment of a new and better order. Gideon's reforming work is not complete when he has thrown down the emblems and instruments of idolatry. This is but half his work. He must next erect an altar to the true God and sacrifice thereon. The danger of every attempted reformation is lest it should stay with the work of destruction—lest the iconoclast should not be also a reformer. It is much easier to throw down than to rebuild. The passions of the destroyer are not always joined to the patient, calm wisdom and energy of the renovator . . . Mere negative Protestantism, negative temperance . . . movements are likely to lead to abortive issues unless they are supplemented by influences which promote and establish positive good. Conviction of sin must be followed by the creation of a new heart if the future life is to be pure . . . it is vain to cast out the evil spirit unless we fill the place of it with a better spirit (Matthew 12:43–45)."

Second, the location of the altar. Gideon was to build this altar to Jehovah "upon the top of this rock" (v. 26). This rock is not to be understood as the rock upon which he put the "present" for the Lord when the Lord first visited him; but rather it is to be understood as a fort, a "stronghold" (Keil). The idea was that the altar was to be public, not secret. Edersheim said the altar was not built "in some secret hiding-place, but on 'the top of this defense [rock]'—either on top of the hill on which the fort stood, or perhaps above the place where the people were wont to seek shelter from the Midianites."

God wants our worship of Him to be obvious. Secret discipleship is unacceptable. "Whosoever therefore shall confess me before men, him will I confess also before my Father which is in heaven" (Matthew 10:32). Unless we have the "before men" in our confession, our confession will not be worth much. Public worship is demanded for a good testimony. The idea that you can stay home and worship by your radio or in front of your television set just as well as in the church is condemned by this vital truth about public worship.

GIDEON

Third, the usage of the altar. The altar was to be used. The building of the altar was to include sacrificing on the altar. Gideon was to sacrifice the "second bullock" on the altar and burn the wood from the image with the sacrifice. This "second bullock" was seven years old which represented the seven years of Midianite oppression. Relief from oppression is thus associated with the sacrifice which pictures Christ. It is the universal message of the cross where the greatest relief from oppression occurs. Burning the wood from the iniquitous image with the sacrifice instructs that the fire of heavenly judgment would purge the land (in this case, first, of Baalism and its altars, then of the Midianites) as the fire of heavenly judgment always does.

2. The Purpose of the Orders

The reason for giving Gideon these orders was to again emphasize a truth we have seen repeatedly emphasized in our previous studies; namely, that if we are going to really solve our problems, we need to deal with the cause of the problem, not just the effect, not just the symptoms. Israel had a great problem with the oppression of the Midianites. For seven years the Midianites had plagued the Israelites, and so much so that they had "greatly impoverished" (6:6) the Israelites. But the Midianites were not Israel's main problem. Their main problem was their forsaking of Jehovah. They had turned from Jehovah to Baal. Because of this, God brought chastisement upon them in the form of the Midianites. Getting rid of the Midianites would not solve their problem. They needed to deal with that which brought the Midianites upon them. "Before we can be delivered from Midian, there must be an honest dealing with the idolatry of evil in the inner life. The altar of Baal must be thrown down, and replaced by the altar of God, and there must be the burnt offering of entire surrender to His claims" (F. B. Meyer).

Many would compromise here, however. They would consent to build the altar of God, but they do not want to give up the altar of Baal. When problems beset such people, they will often come to the pastor for a verse of Scripture and prayer to solve their problems. They allow for the altar of God, but they are unwilling to get rid of the altars of evil at the same time. They do not want the pastor to tell them to give up their evil habits, associations, and philosophies which have caused them their problems. They simply want to combine the altar of God with the altar of evil and think that will solve their problems. But it will not! If you would solve your problems, you must get rid of the altars of evil and replace them with the altar of God. God made it plain to Gideon that it was either God *or* Baal, not God *and* Baal. The altar of Baal must go and the altar of God must be built if the problem of the Midianites is going to be remedied.

3. The Place for the Orders

God's orders for Gideon were to be executed right in his own home. Reformation was to begin on his doorstep where he lived with his father. Before he could lead others to righteousness, he must first be righteous himself. Before he could reform a nation, he must first reform his home. "Is a man going to be a deliverer for all Israel, while his own family is in bondage? Is he to lift up the altar of Jehovah for all Israel, and are those who are nearest and dearest to him to bow to Baal? The circle of divine influence expands from the center. How many are tempted to invert this order. They may be jealous enough for God's altar for all Israel, and yet have never set it up in their own homes. He [who] is too timid to read the word of God and pray with his family; how can he expect liberty and blessing in public prayer?" (Ridout).

This qualification is the basic principle laid down by Christ when He said, "Why beholdest thou the mote that is in thy brother's eye, but considerest not the beam that is in thine own eye? Or how wilt thou say to thy brother, Let me pull out the mote out of thine eye; and, behold, a beam is in thine own eye? Thou hypocrite, first cast the beam out of thine own eye; and then shalt thou see clearly to cast the mote out of thy brother's eye" (Matthew 7:3–5). Gideon must clean up at home before he cleans up a nation. If he will not correct the problems at home, he is not qualified to correct the problems of the nation. "No one is fit for His work in the world till he had begun it in himself and in his own house, and put away all sin and rebellion, however hard the task" (Edersheim).

This place for the orders is spelled out very plainly in regards to the qualification of church officers, too. One of the qualifications for bishops (pastors) is that of ruling well his own house, "For if a man know not how to rule his own house, how shall he take care of the church of God?" (I Timothy 3:5). Likewise deacons are to be "ruling their children and their own houses well" (I Timothy 3:12). If churches followed this vital qualification for office, a great many pastors and deacons would be out of a job; for they definitely do not qualify in this important area. But our churches do not seem to interested in this great principle of starting at home, which probably explains a lot of the problems we have in the church today.

B. THE OBEDIENCE IN THE REFORMATION

Gideon's obedience to God's orders is most inspiring and exemplary. There was promptness, perspiration, and prudence in his obedience.

1. The Promptness in His Obedience

"Then Gideon took ten men of his servants, and did as the LORD had said unto him" (v. 27). "Then" emphasizes the promptness of his obedience. God spoke and Gideon acted. He did not delay, argue, or refuse.

If you would accomplish much in life, you must be punctual to duty. Those who are dilatory will never accomplish a great deal. We see folk all about us who are nothing but floaters. Many church members belong in this category. They never seem to get their life in order. They are sluggish at paying bills, slow at getting assignments done (give them a task at church and you will wait and wait for them to do it—if they even do it), and you are never too sure just when they will show up. They get way behind in their work and complain of a lack of time for everything. But that is not their real problem. They would have plenty of time if they were not so dilatory in performing their responsibilities. Gideon became a great leader of Israel, and one reason is that he did not procrastinate in regard to his duties.

No one can be obedient to the commands of God without being punctual. Every command needs to be followed by a "then." When God gives orders, we do not have the option to wait around and obey when we get good and ready. Timing is so vital, to delay is to lose opportunity.

We often play hypocrite here. We definitely want God to be prompt when we make our petitions known to Him. If God does not act immediately, we often complain and wonder about the faithfulness of God in keeping His prayer promises. But God is always on time; it is we who are dilatory. When God gives us an order, we too often put it off indefinitely until we feel like doing it. But if we want God to hasten our deliverance from the Midianites, we had better be prompt about fulfilling His orders to raze the altar of Baal and raise the altar of Jehovah.

2. The Perspiration in His Obedience

"Gideon took ten men of his servants" to do the job. The task he was assigned by God was not an easy task. The altar of Baal would require great efforts to tear down and destroy. These altars were made of stone and were of large size. Hence, Gideon needed ten of his servants to assist him in accomplishing this work.

This aspect of obedience is too often ignored in our messages. In our eagerness to gain converts and new members in our churches, we often paint Christianity as more of a picnic or vacation than a difficult task. We fail to tell people that obedience is difficult and cannot be done unless we put forth great efforts at times. Therefore, because we have ignored this fact, we have created a generation of soft Christians who do not have the strength or stamina or dedication to oppose even the smallest of temptations, to sacrifice much of their time and possessions, to perform any tasks of Christian service involving hard work, or to even endure a sermon that might go over the thirty minute mark.

Obedience has never been easy. We will find countless things and people that will make obeying God's orders difficult. Friends sometimes make it very difficult to do as God says, and the flesh definitely makes obedience a real struggle. So if we purpose in our heart to obey the Lord, we will have to accept the fact that it will not be easy. But though difficult, the rewards more than compensate for any effort we have expended to obey.

3. The Prudence in His Obedience

"Because he feared his father's household, and the men of the city, that he could not do it by day, that he did it by night" (v. 27). Some might wonder why we put this action of Gideon under "prudence" and not under "cowardliness" or some similar title indicating lack of courage. The answer is that Gideon's fear did not prevent him from doing the task, but it caused him to do the task when it could best be done. There was no disobedience here. His fear simply forced him to exercise wise caution; it did not cause him to become a coward and not tear down the altar of Baal and not make a new altar to Jehovah. Fear does not have to make us cowards. Gideon used fear as it ought to be used—to produce caution in how he did the task to make sure the task was completed as ordered.

If Gideon had proceeded to tear down the altar of Baal in broad daylight, he would have doubtless been stopped by his father's household and the men of the city. When they did discover the destruction of the altar of Baal, they were highly incensed—but the work was done, and they could not stop it then. Had they discovered the work while it was in the process of being done, it is obvious by their reaction that they would have done much to hinder the completion of the work. Thus Gideon "to prevent their resistance in the doing of it [God's orders] . . . prudently chose to do it by night, that he might not be disturbed in these sacred actions" (Matthew Henry).

Therefore, we must not attribute to Gideon a cowardly performance here. Taking ten of his servants and destroying the altar of Baal and then building an altar to Jehovah and sacrificing on it what God instructed was an act of great courage. It was not done without fear, however. But fear only caused him to exercise caution as to when it was done so it could be done. This, of course, does not sanction doing our work undercover when it needs to be done in the open. It only encourages us to be careful that we use wisdom in doing our task so that we successfully outwit the enemy. Our conduct should reflect wisdom, or it will not reflect obedience.

C. THE OPPOSITION TO THE REFORMATION

As we have previously indicated, there was indeed opposition to this reformation which Gideon had instituted. When morning light came, the deed was discovered—and with much indignation. Opposition broke loose which for awhile demanded Gideon's life. "When the men of the city arose early in the morning, behold, the altar of Baal was cast down, and the grove was cut down that was by it, and the second bullock was offered upon the altar that was built. And they said one to another, Who hath done this thing? And when they inquired and asked, they said, Gideon, the son of Joash hath done this thing. Then the men of the city said unto Joash, Bring out thy son, that he may die" (vv. 28–30).

In examining this opposition to Gideon's reformation work, we will note the spurring of the opposition, the seriousness of the opposition, the source of the opposition, and the stopping of the opposition.

1. The Spurring of the Opposition

Opposition occurred when Gideon made a forceful and positive attack on the religion of Baal. This is always the case with opposition from evil. "The world has never loved singularity. Loyalty to conviction, courage to say 'No' to the demands made by fashion and custom, will entail upon you scorn, hardship, hate" (J. D. Jones). However, when the church is dead, when its pulpit lacks an outspoken testimony against wickedness, and when its members' lives are no rebuke to the world about them, then the world will not be hostile to the church. But let the church become vibrant in their faith, let it take strong stands against evil, and let it uphold a high standard of holiness; then the world will show considerable animosity; it will be spurred on to attack and oppose the church. The devil does not waste his time attacking those who are not causing him trouble. But tear down the altar of Baal, and the devil will show up the next morning with blood in his eyes. It is those who "will live godly in Christ Jesus" who "shall suffer persecution" (II Timothy 3:12).

Therefore, when a new pastor comes to a church and wages war against the Baals of the people—e.g. their worldly habits, philosophies, and associations—the congregation will often rise up in force against that Gideon pastor and call for his ouster. But many pastors, who are more interested in having a job than in doing one, find they can get along just fine with the people if they do not attack the altars of Baal and do not insist on giving loyalty to God. In our wicked day a popular minister is seldom a true minister. There is too much sin in the church and in the world for the tearing down of the altars of Baal and the raising up of the altars of God to be applauded. But what schools engaged in preparing men for the ministry speak much about the great opposition the minister will experience if he insists on doing God's work in God's way? Precious few, that's for sure.

2. The Seriousness of the Opposition

The worshippers of Baal insisted that Gideon must die. Opposition does not play games. It is deadly serious. The attack upon righteousness is done with great earnestness. What a great rebuke this is to those who show such lackluster performance in promoting righteousness and in opposing evil. They seem to think we can win the victory over a vicious foe by half-hearted efforts. How foolish to so think, however! The fact that we need to give total effort in our service for God is underscored by the fact that opposition is very earnest. Surely we ought to be as earnest about our cause as evil is about their cause.

This vicious opposition perverted righteousness as evil always does. "By the law of God the worshippers of Baal were to die, but these wicked men impiously turn the penalty upon the worshippers of the God is Israel" (Matthew Henry). This is still done in our day. Notably it is done with our Constitution and the business of the separation of church and state. The Bill of Rights reads under Article One, "Congress shall make no law respecting an establishment of religion, or prohibiting the free exercise thereof." How the wicked pervert that statement from the Constitution! Any reference to God in schools, as an example, is prohibited on the basis of this Article. The wicked never talk about the part of the Article which says Congress is to make no law "prohibiting the free exercise thereof [of religion]." The Article in the Constitution which should protect the free exercise of religion is being used to hinder the free exercise of religion. But that is the way of evil. It perverts, twists, and defiles.

3. The Source of the Opposition

It needs to be pointed out that the first opposition Gideon faced in doing the work of God came from his own people! It did not come first from the Midianites as we would have expected. It was from the people of his own neighborhood, his own relatives, those close to him. It was from the very people who he wanted most to help.

The most difficult opposition a believer experiences is generally from those close to him. The devil knows the best vantage point from which to strike, and so he often strikes from close range. Therefore, opposition is more likely to come from those who profess to be saved, rather than from the ungodly.

Many a pastor will testify that it is not the people outside the church that cause havoc in the church, but it is the church members themselves. And the new converts' strongest and most effective opposition to their faith often comes from their own

GIDEON

family. Close friends, relatives, professing Christians, and fellow church members are often the foremost opposers of true spiritual work, sad to say. Let us be wise to this fact and prepare ourselves for it, so we will not be overly discouraged by such opposition and quit.

4. The Stopping of the Opposition

Opposition to Gideon ran into opposition! Joash, the father of Gideon, came to the defense of Gideon. You would think that Joash would have been the first to be upset. After all, it was his altar that had been torn down; and it was his bullock that had been slain and sacrificed. But in spite of that, he withstood his neighbors and took the part of Gideon. God can raise up supporters for His cause from surprising sources if He so pleases.

Joash cooled down the opposition in two ways: by his challenge for Baal and by his compliment for Gideon.

His challenge for Baal. That which stopped the opposers from pursuing the death of Gideon was a statement by Joash which said, "If he [Baal] be a god, let him plead for himself, because one hath cast down his altar" (v. 31). This statement took vengeance out of the hands of the persecutors and put it into the hands of Baal. It challenged Baal to take action. It indicated that if Baal was of the character his adherents claimed he was, then he could take care of Gideon with dispatch. Joash, of course, implied by the statement that since Gideon had not suffered any evil consequences as a result of tearing down the altar of Baal, these persecutors ought to do some hard thinking about the reality and validity of Baal.

Joash also indicated by this statement that he himself had some misgivings about Baal worship. The action of Gideon obviously encouraged him to make a break with Baal. We never know whom we will influence by our stand for God, but we will influence some. When we take a bold stand for truth and righteousness there will be others who will be encouraged by our stand to also stand. There may not be many who will stand, but count on it that some will. So let us stand true and faithful at all times so others will also be encouraged to godly living.

His compliment for Gideon. "Therefore on that day he called him Jerubbaal, saying, Let Baal plead against him, because he hath thrown down his altar" (v. 32). To further quiet the opposition, Gideon was given a complimentary name by his father. The name was Jerubbaal (Jerubbesheth in II Samuel 11:21). The name characterized Gideon as one who opposed Baal, and it implied that he had done so successfully, for Baal had not shown any retribution upon Gideon. The basic meaning of the name is "let Baal plead" which Jamieson expands as "Jerubbaal . . . with whom Baal contends." Joseph Parker cites the name Jerubbaal as meaning "Baal's antagonists." James Smith in *Handfuls on Purpose* likewise interprets the name as "Baal's antagonist." The name made it clear where Gideon stood, and in accordance with that, Matthew Henry said, "The name was a standing defiance to Baal."

Human nature being what it is, some of Gideon's enemies doubtless spoke the name in derision. Evil always like to snarl out names in derision even if the name has been given in honor. They not only call people bad names, but they also would make a good name sound bad if they can. Joseph Parker, with some sanctified sarcasm, said of this habit of evil men to call good men derisive names, "The least one can do is give a reformer a nickname. If we may not smite him, we may at least throw some appellation at him which we hope the enemy will take up and use as a sting or a thong."

What do people name us? What they name us will tell much about what sort of testimony we have. The "disciples were called Christians [Christ follower] first in Antioch" (Acts 11:26). Though the name was given in derision, it was an honorable name and spoke highly of the disciples; for it indicated they had a good testimony in following Christ. Because of their good testimony, the name is now a most respected name. But when that name was first given, it was meant as a stigma. It was snarled out at the disciples. In fact, the name was seldom used by the disciples themselves in the early church. Tacitus, a Roman historian, writing in the first century said, "The vulgar call them [the disciples] Christians" which certainly underscores the fact that the name was used in a scorning way at first. But the name is no longer a stigma. Even hypocrites like wearing the name. Truth wins out in the long run. Try to stigmatize truth with your nicknames if you like, but those nicknames will in time become names of respect. Righteousness can ennoble the worst of names, but evil will ruin the best of names. What has your life done for your name, for the name of Christ, and for the name of your church?

IV.
Ratification

Judges 6:33–40

When reading about the great saints in the Scripture, we often observe from their experiences that when God calls anyone to service, He will ratify the calling when necessary. This is done in order to give the called ones the assurances they need to pursue their Divine duty. These assurances will fit the assignments; that is, the greater and more unusual the task, the more pronounced and more frequent will be the ratifications.

This ratification practice of God is very evident in Gideon's life. Gideon's task was not the usual day's work. He was called to do the unusual, the exceptional, the abnormal, and for him it was also very unexpected. He was to lead an out-manned Israeli force against the hordes of the Midianites and their allies. So in view of Gideon's calling, it is not surprising that we read of periodic and pronounced ratifications of his calling.

In the passage of Scripture before us, Gideon's call was forcefully ratified by the fortifying of the Spirit, the following of the soldiers, and the fleece of a sheep. These all assured Gideon that he was indeed called of God to deliver Israel from the mighty multitude of the Midianite marauders.

A. THE FORTIFYING OF THE SPIRIT RATIFICATION

The Great Fortifier for a Divine calling is the enduing work of the Holy Spirit. Gideon was not without this work of the Spirit of God, which greatly confirms a calling; for the Scripture says, "the spirit of the Lord came upon Gideon" (v. 34). According to Keil, "came upon Gideon" means the Holy Spirit "clothed, i.e. descended upon him [Gideon], and laid itself around him as it were like a coat of mail, or a strong equipment, so that he became invulnerable and invincible in its might." This word meaning gives us a very instructive description of the fortifying work of the Holy Spirit, and thus it helps us to see plainly the great work this fortifying of the Spirit is to man.

The context of this announcement of the Spirit of God coming upon Gideon reveals to us the instant, indication, and imperativeness of the fortifying.

1. The Instant of the Fortifying

The enduing work of the Spirit occurred right after the Midianites made their annual incursion into the land; for just before the announcement of the Spirit coming upon Gideon, we read, "Then all the Midianites and the Amalekites and children of the east were gathered together, and went over [the Jordan River], and pitched [set up camp] in the valley of Jezreel" (v. 33).

Since it was harvest season—we learned that from Gideon's threshing of wheat (6:11)—it was time for the Midianites and their allies to make their annual invasion into the fertile plain of Esdraelon to plunder the land. But this time, they were not going to be successful in plundering Israel as they had been in the previous seven years. God had called Gideon to lead an attack against the Midianites which would drive them back to their own land. So no sooner had the Midianites invaded, than we read that God countered with "But the spirit of the LORD came upon Gideon" (v. 34). The "Then" of the Midianites was countered with the "But" of God. The enemy invasion signaled the instant for the Spirit of God to come upon Israel's deliverer.

When God's people are willing to serve Him, they can expect the "Then" of the enemy to be countered by a Divine "But." We probably should spell it "Butt" (verb), for that is indeed what it is. God will butt the enemy right back into their own land, and He will do it through a man whom He has just endowed with His Spirit. God is never caught unprepared. He has His men ready the exact instant they are needed. They are fortified by His Spirit to do the job, a fortifying which ratifies their calling.

2. The Indication of the Fortifying

As soon as the Scripture says, "The spirit of the LORD came upon Gideon," it next says, "and he blew a trumpet" (v. 34). This was not a musical celebration. This was the trumpet which called Israel to war to fight the Midianites who had just invaded the land. This blowing of the trumpet was not the only indication of the Spirit coming upon him for his work, but it was the first indication of it recorded in Scripture.

We note two things about this blowing of the trumpet by Gideon: it was an obvious indication and a legitimate indication of the Spirit of God coming upon Gideon.

An obvious indication. Previously, when the Midianites invaded, Gideon, along with other Israelites, had run to their hideouts for fear of the Midianite hordes. Now, however, Gideon stands up to oppose the Midianites and courageously and enthusiastically calls others to come to arms with him. The invasion stirs him mightily—not to run and hide, but to oppose them. He, who formerly was reticent and cowering in seclusion from the Midianites, now under the inspiration of the Spirit of God, puts the trumpet to his lips and gives a mighty blast. A great change has obviously taken place in Gideon, and it was most evident to all.

The same thing happens when God calls men into the ministry today. He endues them with the Holy Spirit to enable them to fulfill their calling. Before their calling they may have given little evidence of their ministry, but when they are called by God and thus endued by the Holy Spirit, evidence will then be obvious. Others will recognize without difficulty the minister's calling. Lack of evidence, however, strongly suggests that one has not been called at all. Unfortunately, the ministry is plagued with this problem.

GIDEON

A legitimate indication. This blowing of the trumpet was a very legitimate indication that the Spirit of God was working in Gideon. Calling Israel to war against Midian was a wise and practical thing to do. When the Spirit of God is working in us we will evidence it in wise and practical conduct.

In contrast to what many think today, the best indication that the Spirit of God is working in us is not some useless babbling in tongues at a church service, but rather it is an inspired and faithful performance in the area of duty. God is not in the business of enduing us with supernatural power for nothing more than a confused yelling experience at church. The Spirit of God comes upon us to do sensible, useful, intelligent, and practical work. It would not have done Israel much good if Gideon had had a twentieth century tongues' experience. But blowing the trumpet to call them to arms was a different story. So was the initial tongues' movement in the New Testament. It was no useless babbling scene. It was a gift to speak in another language, which the speaker previously did not know, in order to facilitate the proclaiming of the Gospel to men of different languages gathered in Jerusalem at that time. Such a tongues' movement, like Gideon's blowing of the trumpet, was practical, sensible, and honored the work of the Spirit of God. Those we have today are nothing of the sort.

3. The Imperativeness of the Fortifying

Gideon certainly could not have fulfilled his calling without the work of the Spirit of God on his behalf. Gideon was called to a work he was not in himself equipped to perform. He did not have the military training and expertise for the task, he did not have the courage and inspiration for the task, and he did not have the position and respect among his fellow men to be a great leader. We would never have picked Gideon for his job; and when we first saw Gideon in Scripture, we were surprised that God picked such a man for the task. But when God fortified Gideon with His Spirit, it helped to ratify his calling by qualifying him to lead Israel. This fortifying endowed him with the gifts, abilities, savvy, courage, and inspiration to do the job. Without the work of the Holy Spirit, Gideon would have been nothing. It was absolutely imperative that "the spirit of God" come upon him if he was to fulfill his calling.

Gideon is not the only one that needs the work of the Spirit of God upon him before he can adequately serve God. We all need this work in order to serve. The greatest of men will be ineffective against the enemy of God's people without the enduing power of the Spirit of God, but the weakest of men will be able to overcome the greatest of enemies when the Spirit of God rests upon him. It is "Not by might [of man], nor by power [of man], but by my spirit, saith the LORD of hosts" (Zechariah 4:6). It is the Spirit that "helpeth our infirmities" (Romans 8:26). He is the One Who gives us our greatest help, our greatest fortifying, our greatest strengthening for our task. But if we are unwilling to surrender to the will of God, we will greatly hinder the work of the Spirit in us. Therefore, if we want the all important working of the Holy Spirit in us, let us heed Paul's words which warn us to "Grieve not the holy Spirit of God" (Ephesians 4:30), and "Quench not the Spirit" (I Thessalonians 5:19).

B. THE FOLLOWING OF THE SOLDIERS' RATIFICATION

If Gideon is going to lead the Israelites against the Midianite hordes, he will have to experience acceptance by others. Others will have to follow him—and they did. When he blew the trumpet and sent messengers to his people, they responded well to his call to arms; and they readily recognized him as their captain. This enthusiastic following of Gideon by the soldiers was another ratification of his calling from God.

1. The Response to His Call to Arms

Gideon issued a call to arms to those people and tribes whose land included or bordered the Jezreel valley; and who were, therefore, the most afflicted by the invasion of the Midi-

Gideon

anites. These invaders had understandably come to some of the most fruitful land in Israel when they came to the valley of Jezreel to plunder the Israelites.

But this valley area, also known as the plain of Esdraelon, is not only one of the most fruitful spots in Israel, it is also one of the great battlegrounds of the ages. With the famous town of Megiddo on the western side of the area and Jezreel on the east, this valley, where Gideon will rout the Midianites, is the place of a number of most significant battles. About 1500 B.C. it was the scene of the famous battle between the Syrian states and Egypt then ruled by Thutmose III. It was the battleground where Barak defeated Sisera (Judges 4,5). It was where Saul was slain in his last battle against the Philistines (I Samuel 31). It was in this area where Jehu killed Joram, king of Israel, Ahaziah, king of Judah, and wicked Jezebel, who died an ignominious death in the streets of Jezreel (II Kings 9:14–37). It is also where King Joash was slain by Pharaoh-necho (II Kings 23:28–30). And, of special significance to us today, it is this area where the last great battle of the ages, known as Armageddon, will be fought (Revelation 16:12–16).

Living in and around this valley, in Gideon's time, was half the tribe of Manasseh (the half which was located on the west side of the Jordan), the family of Abiezer of the tribe of Manasseh (Gideon's family), the tribes of Zebulun and Naphtali (they were on the north side of the valley), and the tribe Asher (they were on the west side of the valley). To these Gideon extended the call to arms, and each tribe responded well. They quickly assembled together to battle the Midianites. "Abiezer was gathered after him. And he sent messengers throughout all Manassah, who also was gathered after him: and he sent messengers unto Asher, and unto Zebulun, and unto Naphtali; and they came up to meet them" (vv. 34–36). The tribe of Issachar, which was right in the midst of the valley, was not extended a call. They probably could not have responded anyway, for the Midianites encamped in most of their land, which would make assembling of troops nigh unto impossible.

Ratification

We would expect the tribe of Zebulun and Naphtali to respond well, for they were a gallant people described as those "who jeoparded their lives unto the death in the high places of the field" (Judges 5:18) in Israel's last great war when Barak and Deborah led them against Sisera. But we would not expect Asher and the family of Abiezer to respond to the call to arms. Asher had especially been singled out by Deborah in her song, after that victorious war against Sisera, as those who "continued on the seashore, and abode in his breaches [inlets]" (Judges 5:17). They had refused to go to battle. There are always some in every age who prefer their ease and pleasures to patriotic sacrifice. They want the fruits of victorious warfare, but they do not want to sacrifice to gain the victory. But now they respond to Gideon's call and show up for the battle. The other unexpected responders to the call to arms, the Abiezerites, had just a few days earlier been clamoring for Gideon's neck. But things have changed with them, too. So with one accord, they, along with all the other people, come together to war against the Midianites.

God was working in the hearts of all these tribes and people. They are ready to do battle with the enemy. They are ready to oppose evil as it ought to be opposed. Such an attitude not only gave encouraging ratification to Gideon of his calling, but it was also greatly needed if Gideon was to successfully lead Israel against Midian. It is very difficult for any man, as many pastors will testify, to successfully get the enemy out of God's land, or out of God's church, unless God's people are of the attitude to rise up and vigorously oppose the enemy.

2. The Recognition of His Captaincy of the Army

The people summoned to fight the Midianites not only responded favorably to the call to go to war against Midian, but they also "gathered after him" (vv. 34,35). They were not only ready to go to war, but they were also ready to acknowledge Gideon as their captain. Such a unanimous recognition of his leadership was indeed a ratification for Gideon that God had called him. He needed that recognition, or he could not have fulfilled his calling. Such a recognition in itself does not necessarily confirm a Divine calling, for many people rally around devilish leaders; but in this case, considering the circumstances, the rallying around Gideon did plainly ratify his calling.

All of this is a great encouragement to anyone called of God to lead men in His service. Like Gideon, most are called before they have the acceptance of the people. And, like Gideon, a good number are called when their circumstances would argue against the call. They are unknown and hence unrecognized. How they will ever be noticed and acknowledged is the question which seems at times to have no answer. But "how strikingly does the experience of Gideon, at this stage of his story, prove that no man who is conscious of being endowed with superior natural talents in combination with high moral principle should allow himself to be discouraged even though for a season he may fail to be duly appreciated by his fellow men. Let him 'bide his time'" (W. W. Duncan), and he will be duly recognized and put in position. Therefore, "it is at once the duty and the interest of every one . . . to go straight forward in the improvement of all his talents and opportunities, and in the pursuit and practice of what is right, heedless of what men may say or do, satisfied that in due time God will secure for him the very place which it is fittest and best that he should occupy, in spite of all the opposition of earth or hell" (Ibid.).

How often great men were passed over, ignored, and voted against before they did a great work. But that has not stopped the work, for if God wants you in some area of service and has endowed you to perform that service, He will put you there in due time. He can put you in places you could not possibly obtain yourself and in places you never dreamed possible. You do not have to work under the table or behind people's backs or pull strings in order to get a place in His vineyard. All you need to do is surrender to His will and prepare faithfully for His service. When it is time for you to be placed in His service, God will place you where He wants you to serve. So, lowly Gideon, who just days earlier was so rejected that people were clamoring for his neck, now is recognized enthusiastically by the people of Israel. It certainly was an encouraging ratification of his call, and it is also a great encouragement to any who are conscious of God's call but are still in an obscure place and rejected by man.

C. THE FLEECE OF A SHEEP RATIFICATION

After the soldiers from the various tribes had assembled together at Gideon's call to arms, Gideon went to God in prayer. He made a request for God to give a sign to ratify his calling again. He prayed, "If thou wilt save Israel by mine hand, as thou has said, Behold, I will put a fleece of wool in the floor; and if the dew be on the fleece only, and it be dry upon all the earth beside [it], then shall I know that thou wilt save Israel by mine hand, as thou hast said" (vv. 36,37). When this happened as Gideon proposed, he then reversed the conditions of the sign and prayed, "Let not thine anger be hot against me, and I will speak but this once: let me prove, I pray thee, but this once more with the fleece; let it now be dry only upon the fleece, and upon all the ground let there be dew" (v. 39). Gideon's prayer was answered, for "God did so that night: for it was dry upon the fleece only, and there was dew on all the ground" (v. 40). Gideon's call was again ratified.

This fleece ratification is the most famous of all the many confirmations which Gideon experienced for his calling. So familiar, in fact, are people with this fleece sign, that it is common for folk to say "we have thrown out the fleece" when they are seeking some outward sign to indicate or confirm the will of God for their lives.

In reading what others have written on Gideon's fleece sign experience, one finds a mixture of conclusions as to the character of Gideon's request. Some believe Gideon was acting entirely in the flesh when he sought this sign from God. They want to condemn Gideon for his request, and condemn all pursuit of signs. They put him in the category of those whom Christ condemned for seeking a sign when He said, "An evil and adulterous generation seeketh after a sign" (Matthew 12:39). As

GIDEON

Wiseman notes, "The story of Gideon and his fleece is one of those which a certain class of Christians would desire to see expunged from the sacred volume." I. M. Haldeman is one who really condemns Gideon's request for a sign. He said, "It proved that Gideon's heart was still full of unbelief . . . the demand for signs is simply a mode of unbelief, and . . . instead of leading to faith in the things of God, it only strengthens the unbelief, makes the Christian more critical, more doubtful, and more demanding for even stronger evidence that shall appeal to sight."

Others would completely exonerate Gideon. One writer in *Pulpit Commentary* makes the pursuit of the sign a noble character trait when he says, "In his humility he [Gideon] craves a sign that he is indeed chosen and called" (A. C. Hervey). Edersheim so exonerates Gideon that he does not allow for a fault of any kind in Gideon's action. He says, "It was not from unbelief, nor yet in weakness of faith, that Gideon asked a sign from the Lord." Some, in their effort to exonerate Gideon's actions here, insist Gideon sought the sign to convince others of his calling. As an example, *The New Scofield Reference Bible* has a footnote which says one of the reasons for the fleece was to give "evidence that would convince the people that he [Gideon] was really God's instrument." However, Scripture does not give the slightest warrant for such a conclusion. Gideon's prayer was, "then shall I [not others] know that thou wilt save Israel by mine hand" (v. 37). The emphasis was on Gideon being assured. Nothing was said about others being assured or even aware of this sign. It was "I" not the people.

In due respect to these deservedly respected sources whom we have just quoted, we do not believe Gideon should be either totally condemned or totally exonerated in his sign seeking with the fleece. We believe there is both weakness and strength, both the flesh and the spirit, both faith and unbelief in Gideon's action in this sign seeking experience. So as we examine this experience of Gideon, we will not only commend some of his action in seeking the sign; but we will also condemn some of his action. All of this will guide us in how we apply Gideon's sign seeking conduct to our own lives.

We will note six things about Gideon's action in seeking this sign involving the fleece to ratify his calling as Israel's deliverer from Midian. We will note that Gideon asked for the sign unnecessarily, reverently, impartially, inappropriately, successfully, and honestly.

1. He Asked Unnecessarily

Was Gideon's call so vague and uncertain at this time that he needed a sign to again confirm it? Not at all! Gideon did not need more signs to ratify the fact that he was to lead Israel in battle against Midian. He had already been given significant assurances of the validity of his calling. In the initial revelation of "the angel of the LORD" to him, he had asked and received ample confirmation of the validity of the revelation and call. Again in this chapter, we have seen his call ratified in the Spirit of God coming upon him and in the response of the people to his call to arms and to his captaincy of the army. Gideon had both the Word of God and circumstances to substantially verify the call. So he was indeed at fault in asking for a sign. He did not need any more signs to give proof that "as thou has said" (vv. 36, 37) was indeed going to happen.

Before we begin asking God for signs about whether we should do this or that, we need to ask whether or not we really need more confirmation. Sometimes instead of more confirmation, we just need to sit down and take stock of all the things which have already ratified a course of action. God has given us many precepts and principles in the Word of God—and much more than Gideon ever had—to guide our thinking. We can interpret our circumstances and our inspirations with these precepts and principles to know God's will. Many, however, are like Gideon in that they are ever asking for more signs when they already have enough. Their problem is not lack of proof but a lack of pondering all the obvious indications they have in hand regarding a particular course of action.

2. He Asked Reverently

Though he did not need to ask for more signs, yet when he did ask, the manner in which Gideon approached God about the sign certainly was not irreverent. He did not speak in sneering, scornful ways. Rather, Gideon showed a good healthy respect of God. This is especially seen in his second request, when reversing the condition of the sign. When addressing God then, he seemed very concerned that he might be offending God. "Gideon said unto God, Let not thine anger be hot against me, and I will speak but this once" (v. 39). That is definitely not the language of irreverence. Gideon did indeed have some faults in this sign asking, but one of them was not irreverence.

There is no question that in the New Testament Christ really denounced some who were unnecessarily seeking signs from Him. When He said, "An evil and adulterous generation seeketh after a sign" (Matthew 12:39), He spoke with fire. But these remarks were in reference to the ungodly whose every request for a sign was full of sneering scorn. These folks dogged His path and even showed up at the cross where they continued their irreverent behavior. They "reviled him, wagging their heads, And saying . . . If thou be the Son of God, come down from the cross" (Matthew 27:39,40), and "mocking, said . . . Let Christ the King of Israel descend now from the cross, that we may see and believe" (Mark 15:31,32). But they would not have believed Him if He had come down from the cross in a dramatic demonstration of power. They had not believed any of the many previous signs He had given, and they would not believe at the cross. They gave away their wicked unbelieving hearts by their irreverence towards Him. As a result, they are to be totally condemned in their action. But Gideon was different, for he approached God with much reverence when he sought another sign of confirmation.

It makes a great deal of difference in how one makes a request as to whether that action will produce good or evil. We may not always make requests for the right things, but we can always make the request in the right way—by showing due respect of God. Lack of reverence for God will greatly hinder even a legitimate request, but where reverence is present, a faulty request will not jeopardize one's fellowship with God. We need to examine our requests to see if they are proper, but, more importantly, we need first to examine our respect for God. If our respect for God is right, our requests will eventually become right.

3. He Asked Impartially

Gideon's first request was for God to cause the dew to come upon the fleece only. This happened. However, Gideon did not stop there. He then asked God to cause the dew to be on everything but the fleece. While this second request may on the surface look like it was a rejection of the first sign, it actually was a test of the sign. "Wool generally attracts the dew, even when other objects remain dry" (Keil). Therefore, Gideon, to make sure the first sign was not just a natural occurrence, reversed the stipulation. This was a wise thing to do. It showed impartiality. It said he was not trying to ask for a sign that would normally happen in the way he wanted it to happen. He was fair in the way he asked for the fleece sign.

Too often the asking of signs by people today is conspicuously carnal because the asker conjures up a sign that would normally occur anyway. It, therefore, is not a fair test. It does not validate anything. If you are afraid to test the sign by reversing the conditions of a sign or by some other equitable stipulation, then you are not being impartial and will therefore not get a valid indication from your sign. If you control the sign to make it do what you want it to do, then it is no longer a valid sign. The stipulations of the sign must be impartial or the sign loses it validity.

4. He Asked Inappropriately

The sign requested was inappropriate because it was unrelated in a practical and logical way to his calling. To illustrate what we mean here, let us go to Genesis 24 and consider Abraham's servant when he went to seek a wife for Isaac. When he arrived in the city of Nahor, he asked for a sign. He said, "Let it come to pass, that the damsel to whom I shall say, Let down thy pitcher, I pray thee, that I may drink; and she shall say, Drink, and I will give thy camels drink also: let the same be she that thou hast appointed for thy servant Isaac; and thereby shall I know that thou hast shown kindness unto my master" (Genesis 24:14). Now this was a very appropriate sign. Why? Because it would reveal the character of the woman, and the character of the woman was indeed a very important sign as to whether or not she should be Isaac's wife. Some of the character revealed here was her unselfishness and her consideration of the needs of others—she gave the servant a drink and offered to water his camels; industriousness—she watered the camels which was very hard work; and faithfulness—she could keep her word. She said she would water the camels until they finished drinking (Genesis 24:19), and she did (Genesis 24:22). Camels drink a lot of water, and Abraham's servant had ten camels (Genesis 24:10) to water. This would really test her regarding keeping her word. So this sign, which Abraham's servant used to determine the right woman for Isaac, was very appropriate. The sign was related to the case and it was practical.

Our sign seeking should not be the putting out of some fleece that has nothing to do with the area in which we want confirmation. God had not been that way in giving Gideon ratifications of His will. He had given Gideon confirmation by (1) turning the present into a sacrifice—thus verifying Divine behavior and proving to Gideon in a logical way that He was God; (2) endowing Gideon with the Spirit of God—a great necessity for his work; and (3) causing the people to respond to Gideon's call to arms and to Gideon as their captain. These were logical signs, practical signs, and sensible signs. Fleece and dew, to the contrary, were not as appropriate. They, therefore, do not constitute a pattern for us to follow. They are not the normal, recommended, or wise way of discovering or ratifying the will of God.

5. He Asked Successfully

God gave Gideon the sign he requested. But this does not prove that Gideon's request was therefore without any fault. Rather it shows us how the grace of God responds to one whose faith is weak and who, though faulty, is seeking to strengthen that faith.

Gideon was in the category of a new convert when he made this request. He had only been a few days in his new position and persuasions. We are most uncharitable if we expect anyone to grow to maturity overnight. Gideon was still growing in the faith, and so facing the great multitude of Midianites was not easy. He wanted more help for his faith. Christ's attitude towards the weak in faith will be found in the statement He quoted from Isaiah concerning His action toward the weak in faith: "A bruised reed shall he not break, and smoking flax shall he not quench, till he send forth judgment unto victory" (Matthew 12:20). As Matthew Henry said, "See how tender God is of true believers though they be weak, and how ready to condescend to their infirmities, that the bruised reed may not be broken nor the smoking flax quenched."

We must be careful here, however, that we do not interpret God's accommodating of Gideon's request as a blanket approval of all sign requests. God's helping of the feeble does not justify the continuance of our remaining weak. Baby talk is cute in babies, but it is disgusting in adults. The same is true spiritually.

So let us not use the weakness of another to justify our weakness. We will discover that God will not respond so favorably to sign asking when we do not act according to the light we walk in. And we walk in more, tremendously more, light than Gideon ever did.

6. He Asked Honestly

When the sign experience was completed, Gideon did not ask again for more ratification. He accepted the ratification of his calling and pursued the fulfilling of that calling. Such an acceptance of the sign will exempt Gideon from the charge of "evil and adulterous generation" (Matthew 12:39), and refutes the charge which Haldeman made; namely, "It proved that Gideon's heart was still full of unbelief . . . the demand for signs is simply a mode of unbelief, and . . . instead of leading to faith in the things of God, it only strengthens the unbelief."

Many ask for signs; but when they turn out in a different way than they want them to, they reject them. Such folk are not honest at all in their sign seeking; and when integrity is lacking, the pursuit of signs is bogus from beginning to end. Gideon, however, was honest; and so when the sign was given the two times regarding the dew and the fleece, he accepted it. He may have wished to be exempted from the call he was given which was to lead the Israelites into the rugged battle of the Midianites, but he abided by what the sign said. It was a great display of integrity.

V.
REDUCTION

JUDGES 7:1–8

HOURS BEFORE THE great battle against Midian was to begin, Gideon learned a Divine principle which was repeated by Christ in the New Testament. The principle was: "Many be called, but few chosen" (Matthew 20:16). When Gideon blew his trumpet to call Israel to battle, 32,000 showed up (v. 3). But of that number, only 300 were chosen by God to actually lead the attack against Midian.

The Divinely ordered reduction of Gideon's army took place when Gideon was positioning his army for the battle against the Midianites. After the final fleece sign, Gideon "rose up early [a commendable notation about Gideon's lifestyle—late rising, unless one has been on a night shift, is generally indicative of poor character], and pitched [stationed his army] beside [in the vicinity of] the well of Harod: so that the host of the Midianites were on the north side of them, by the hill of Moreh, in the valley" (v. 1). Gideon's army was on the hill, and "the host of Midian was beneath him in the valley" (v. 8). Things were all set for the battle against Midian. But just then, Gideon heard from God about the reduction plan for the army.

God's orders to reduce the size of Gideon's army certainly had to be a surprise for Gideon. Though 32,000 had heeded Gideon's call, it was still a small army compared to Midian's army which had 135,000 troops (Judges 8:10). Natural man would seek an increase in the size of his army, not a decrease. But surprised as he may have been at the orders to reduce the size of his army, Gideon did not hesitate to do as God commanded. As soon as he was given instructions on how to reduce the number in his army, he immediately went to work to do as God had ordered. Gideon's faith was growing. He was no longer disputing with God, but now took Him at His Word in spite of the unexpected nature of the command. Would that all of us were so prompt and uncontesting in obeying God's orders.

In this study of the reduction of the numbers in Gideon's army, we will consider the purpose of the reduction, the program for the reduction, and the promise in the reduction.

A. THE PURPOSE OF THE REDUCTION

When God informed Gideon that his army needed to be reduced in size, He did not leave him in the dark as to why it needed to be reduced. God said, "The people that are with thee are too many for me to give the Midianites into their hands, lest Israel vaunt themselves against me, saying, Mine own hand hath saved me" (v. 2). Pride was the reason why the army needed to decrease in size, and "Nothing develops a nation's pride like military success" (*Biblical Illustrator*). Pride was as much, if not more, of an enemy of Israel than was Midian. God viewed it as such a great peril to Israel that He ordered a reduction in the size of Israel's army even though it was outnumbered more than four to one by the Midianite hordes.

Only God would get this concerned about pride. Mankind certainly does not see pride as a great peril. In fact, we speak very benevolently about pride today. Man is encouraged to brag and boast about his achievements—past, present, and future. If one does not boast, he is often viewed by the world as having some sort of success-inhibiting complex. But regardless of what man says of pride, God looks upon it as great evil. In the reduction announcement to Gideon, God states two serious problems with pride: the emphasis of pride ("vaunt themselves") and the enmity of pride ("against me [God]").

1. The Emphasis of Pride

"Vaunt themselves" is always the chief emphasis of pride.

REDUCTION

Pride delights in the exalting of self. It fosters self-centeredness, self-love, self-importance, and a host of other self-exalting attitudes. Pride is a production which features self as the star. Pride makes self the hero of every episode. When a person puts the emphasis on self, they only reveal they are filled with pride.

With emphasis on self, pride has a perverted view of both salvation and service.

Pride has a perverted view of salvation. Israel needed to be and would be delivered by God from the Midianite oppression. However, if their army was not reduced in size at this time, pride would cause them to think they had delivered themselves.

This is a universal problem with man. Especially in the matter of soul salvation does the pride of man have a problem here. Natural man despises grace. It is his pride which causes him to think he can work his way to heaven. But Scripture plainly states, "For by grace are ye saved through faith; and that not of yourselves: it is a gift of God: Not of works, lest any man should boast" (Ephesians 2:8,9). There will be no braggarts in heaven, and God did not want any in Israel either after the deliverance from Midian. He wants Israel to see that it was God Who saved them from the hand of the Midianites. Therefore, the army will have to be reduced in size to eliminate pride. Then Israel will readily recognize it was God, not their own efforts, that wrought their salvation.

Pride has a perverted view of service. God could whip the Midianites with or without the army of Israel. "There is no restraint to the LORD to save by many or by few" (I Samuel 14:6). But if the army is not reduced in size, the soldiers will get puffed up and think they won the victory for God, rather than the other way around; for pride views our service as needful for God if He is going to accomplish anything on earth. It thinks God cannot get along without our help; when, in truth, we cannot get along without God's help. "Except the LORD build the house, they labour in vain that build it: except the LORD keep the city, the watchman waketh but in vain" (Psalm 127:1).

Pride forgets that service is a privilege. God does not need us at all, but He gives us a place of service for our own blessing. Away with the idea we are indispensable to God. Count service not as a favor for God, but as God doing a favor for us.

2. The Enmity of Pride

Pride is "against God." Pride always opposes God. Satan's great problem was pride, and it turned him against God. It was pride which was a great factor in getting Adam and Eve to disobey the Word of God in the Garden of Eden. Israel had already suffered miserably for seven years at the hands of the Midianites, because they had opposed God in favor of Baal. They did not need anymore turning against God. Therefore, the number in the army must be severely reduced to prevent pride in the hearts of the Israelites; otherwise Israel would turn against God and turn victory into defeat.

How often when an organization grows in size, it grows increasingly antagonistic towards God. The greater the population of our nation, the more opposed to God we have become. The more students a college gains, the more it seems to drift from the truth and become at enmity with God. When Yale, as an example, was small, they were on good terms with God. But today Yale is a large university and exceedingly opposed to God. Many of our Christian schools today are showing the same trend. When they were small, they were loyal to God's Word. But with a considerable growth in the number of students, the schools have begun to drift from the truth. Instead of supporting the Scripturally declared standards of God, they now oppose them. Churches are not exempted in this problem of pride either. Many churches when small and despised were loyal to God; but when their membership increased greatly, we soon heard of variances in their moral and doctrinal positions. With the passing of years, they slowly but surely turned against God and became apostate. Pride is one of the great causes of apostasy. Pride always turns against God.

Reduction

The great peril of pride certainly justifies the reduction of Israel's army even though to natural man it seemed unwise and strange to do. Would that we were not afraid to take drastic action, if necessary, in order to prevent pride from becoming a problem in our life.

B. THE PROGRAM FOR THE REDUCTION

Gideon did not have to wonder long how he was going to reduce the size of his army. As soon as God told him *why* the army needed to be reduced in size, He next told him *how* it was to be reduced in size. Two tests were to be given the soldiers: the test of dread and the test of drinking. These tests would thin the ranks to a number which would prevent pride from becoming a problem in the victory over Midian.

1. The Test of Dread

The first test the soldiers were given would reveal who was afraid and who was not. God said to Gideon, "Go to, proclaim in the ears of the people, saying, Whosoever is fearful and afraid [means to tremble, and interestingly and fittingly comes from same root as 'Harod,' the name of the well around which the army was gathered], let him return and depart early from Mount Gilead" (v. 3). This test was very effective in reducing the numbers in the army; for as a result of the test, "there returned of the people twenty and two thousand" (Ibid.) of the original thirty-two thousand soldiers.

This test of dread was not a new test for soldiers in Israel's military, for God had given Moses similar instructions when Israel was in the wilderness. God said, "When thou goest out to battle against thine enemies, and seest horses, and chariots, and a people more than thou, be not afraid of them: for the LORD thy God is with thee . . . What man is there that is fearful and fainthearted? let him go and return unto his house, lest his brethren's heart faint as well as his heart" (Deuteronomy 20:1, 8). If an Israelite was too afraid to fight, he was discharged from the military.

Gideon

God was not only stopping pride by reducing the size of Gideon's army, but He was also strengthening the army by preventing it from being crippled by fear. Fear spreads like wildfire. With so many being greatly afraid, it could have quickly paralyzed Gideon's army. This is something astute military leaders have always known. As an example, Scipio, a Roman general of centuries past, understood well this problem of fear. When he discovered there were some three hundred Sicilian horsemen in his group that were terrified at going to war against Carthage, he would not let them go into battle with him against Carthage. He knew that these horsemen, with their evident fear, could cause great problems for the morale of his troops; therefore, he wisely kept them from the fight even though it reduced his numbers.

This problem of fear also shows up in the church. Maclaren said, in reference to the fearful being removed from Gideon's army, "Why were the 'fearful' dismissed? Because fear is contagious; and, in undisciplined armies like Gideon's, panic, once started, spreads swiftly, and becomes frenzied confusion. The same thing is true in the work of the church today. Who that has had much to do with guiding its operations has not groaned over the dead weight of the timid and sluggish souls, who see difficulties and never the way to get over them? . . . Cowardice, dressed up as cautious prudence, weakens the efficiency of every regiment in Christ's army." Ridout notes, "Ah, are there not many in our day who see the path of testimony and conflict, and have not the courage to take it? We fear persecution, we fear scorn, we fear what the world will say. Then, alas, we are not ready for God to use, and must stand aside." Another good comment along this line comes from W. W. Duncan who says, "Too many professed followers of Christ . . . are ready enough to cast in their lot with Him so long as there is no immediate appearance of suffering or of sacrifice for His name's sake, but who, the moment that real danger stares them in the face, take the earliest opportunity of slinking away and renouncing the principles to which they formerly in words adhered. Such disciples are totally unworthy of the name. They are not good soldiers of the Cross. They are devoid of the sterling principle which is essential to constancy and success in the Christian warfare—mere 'carpet knights,' who 'make a fair show in the flesh,' flourishing their trumpets and brandishing their weapons when there is no foe with whom to contend, but . . . altering their whole tone and demeanor whenever circumstances occur which put their sincerity to the proof."

Yes, many a church member and many a pastor have let fear dictate their convictions, their stand, their message. Such folk are a great hindrance to doing the work of God, and they need to be dismissed from the ranks. We are better off without them even if their dismissal severely reduces our numbers.

2. The Test of Drinking

The second test was a very unique but effective test. After twenty-two thousand had left the army as a result of the test of dread, God said to Gideon, "The people are yet too many; bring them down unto the water [to drink], and I will try them for thee there . . . Every one that lappeth of the water with his tongue, as a dog lappeth, him shalt thou set by himself [to remain in the army]; likewise every one that boweth down upon his knees to drink [will be excluded from the army]" (vv. 4,5). The manner in which the soldiers drank water was the final test to reduce the ranks of the army. This test nearly depleted the army entirely, for only three hundred were left after the test. "The number of them that lapped, putting their hand to their mouth, were three hundred" (v. 6).

Again, as we noted in the first test, while the reduction of the army was primarily to stop pride, it also eliminated some other undesirable situations. The dread test eliminated the problem of the fearful and fainthearted. Now the drinking test eliminated those who were careless and lacked caution, who gave themselves too freely and unguardingly to the fulfilling of the appetites of the flesh. God was literally purifying the army with the drinking test, for the word "try" (v. 4) is the "The word used for refining metals by separating the dross from pure ore" (F. C. Cook).

The two styles of drinking need to be examined here to appreciate the conclusions we have made. To lap up water as a dog was the method of cupping the hands and putting them into the stream or well of water and then bringing them to the mouth and lapping the water out of the hand. This "mode of drinking water . . . is still common in India and other parts of the east, where men can drink in this way with a rapidity which astonishes a European" (Wiseman). The other form of drinking—that which resulted in a discharge from Gideon's army—was to bow down towards the water and put your face in the water and drink. As can be easily observed, one method allowed for the drinker to be very careful and conscious of what was going on around him when he was drinking; but the other method put the drinker at the mercy of his surroundings, for he gave himself totally to drinking.

Since these soldiers were not far from the Midianites when they drank this water, they needed to be on guard when drinking. But only three hundred of them demonstrated good soldiery by being cautious and careful when they drank the water. They never let down their guard. Quenching their thirst was not so important that they would drop their guard against the Midianites. The other nine thousand seven hundred threw caution to the wind and gave themselves wholly to drinking. "They who threw themselves on the ground and drank freely were the more self-indulgent; while they who, remembering the near presence of the enemy, slaked their thirst with moderation without being off their guard for an instant, were the true soldiers of the army of God" (F. C. Cook).

There are several helpful lessons which can be learned from this test. First, we learn about an important requirement of a good soldier of Jesus Christ. Second, we learn about the revealing of our character in small matters.

The requirement of a good soldier. "Among all the qualities needed in a soldier of Jesus Christ, none perhaps is more important than a certain command of one's self, a certain keeping of the body under" (Edward B. Mason). We must never allow our physical appetites, though legitimate as they may be, to cause us to let down our spiritual guard. The giving of ourselves in an abandoned way to the appetites of the flesh is a peril that will destroy the best of men. As James Smith said, "We are not fit for the work of God while our own personal comfort is our chief concern . . . We don't live to eat and drink; we eat and drink that we may live to the glory of our God." Ridout says, "It is necessary to quench the thirst, but it must not be such an absorbing necessity that it takes the chief place. The needs of this life are evident, but are they chief with us?" And Maclaren says, "Life is to some men first a place for strenuous endeavor, and only secondly a place of refreshment. Such think of duty first and of water afterwards. To them all the innocent joys and pleasures of the natural life are as brooks by the way, of which Christ's soldier should drink, mainly that he may be reinvigorated for conflict. There are others whose conception of life is a scene of enjoyment, for which work is unfortunately a necessary but disagreeable preliminary."

It is very apparent today that many church members belong in the nine thousand seven hundred group; for, like the world, most of these members have no higher goals than satisfying their fleshly appetites. So fleshly appetites are championed and made all-important while spiritual pursuits and duties are given a back seat. These members make a career out of what should be only a pastime. Recreation is made a vocation, and pleasure seeking is given priority over church services. Yes, many in the church have their face buried in the water in a careless and inordinate pursuit of the things of the flesh. And it has cost them plenty in the area of service for God; for it has disqualified them from God's army, like it did the nine thousand seven hundred.

The revelation of character. From this drinking test, we observe that important character traits are often readily revealed by trifling matters. Jesus said, "He that is faithful in that which is least is faithful also in much: and he that is unjust in the least is unjust also in much" (Luke 16:10). "Many are the commonplace incidents, the seemingly small points in life, that test the quality of men. Everyday we are led to the stream-side to show what we are, whether eager in Divine enterprise of faith or slack . . . We show our spiritual state by the way in which we spend our leisure" (R. A. Watson).

This fact—that little actions betray our character—is well illustrated by the story told of a man being considered for a promotion. He was taken to lunch in a cafeteria by the one who could promote him. Going through the line, the man took an extra pat of butter and concealed it under one of his plates, so the check-out girl would not see it and charge him for it. His superior, seeing this bit of dishonesty, decided then and there that the man was not a good one to promote. It was only a small theft, true; but it revealed a major defect in his character.

We must discipline every facet of our life, though small and trifling it may seem to us, if we are going to have the sterling character needed to serve well in God's army. If we think we do not have to practice our faith in the small areas of our life, we will soon discover that we will not do well in practicing our faith in the great areas of our life. A large rope is made up of many small strands. If the small strands are defective, the entire rope will be defective. So it is with character. If the small areas of life are not sound, the large areas will not be sound either.

C. THE PROMISE IN THE REDUCTION

When there remained but three hundred men of the original thirty-two thousand, God said to Gideon, "By the three hundred men that lapped will I save you, and deliver the Midianites into thine hand" (v. 7). What a great promise! We will note the timing of the promise and the teaching of the promise.

1. The Timing of the Promise

The promise regarding the future success of Gideon's army

REDUCTION

did not come until after the army of thirty-two thousand was reduced, in adherence to God's orders, by thirty-one thousand seven hundred soldiers. Before Gideon was given a great promise, he had to first demonstrate great obedience. Obedience secured the promise.

Obedience will sooner or later make the promises of God more real, more clear, and more definite. But obedience is not always easy. It will test our faith to the limit at times. Obedience sometimes seems as though it is leading us to the place where there are no promising prospects. When Gideon saw his army dwindle down to only a few hundred, it would be hard for the natural eye to be encouraged about prospects. And when we come to a place like that in our obedience, the devil often comes along and tries to use the difficulty of the hour to cause us to throw in the towel, give up our faith, and forsake obedience. But if we are going to succeed in doing God's work and discover His great promises, we must obey by faith, not by sight. We may have to see our earthly prospects reduced from thirty-two thousand to but three hundred before the reward of faith begins to shine through the darkness of our circumstances. But it will shine through.

2. The Teaching of the Promise

Loudly and clearly this promise says quality is more important than quantity. Therefore, this whole reduction plan, with its cli-mactic promise, should make us wary of all the emphasis on numbers in our churches. We nearly worship numbers in church today. "There is a subtle desire for numbers with us all . . . [but] Numbers have too often been the occasion for the pride that goeth before destruction . . . Better far the little company, tried and tested by God Himself, than the large and respectable body which commands respect in the eyes of the world by its numbers" (Ridout).

Our large churches, with their great emphasis on numbers, could substantially reduce their numbers and not lose a whit spiritually. In the quest for numbers, many of these churches have ignored character. They boast and brag on how many conversions and baptisms they have, but they pass over the fact that many of those who make decisions and are baptized are as phony as a three dollar bill. Some fundamental churches who lead the nation in conversion and baptism decisions seem never to gain much from them. We personally knew of a church which boasted of several thousand converts a year—which was what their Sunday School attendance average was year after year. To question their claim or other churches' claims of many professions is to receive a sharp retort of "show me your statistics and then I will talk about what happens to mine." This retort, however, is nothing but a dishonest cover-up of the fact that much of their work is superficial and aimed at obtaining statistics more than winning any spiritual battles. Pride oozes out of every announcement these number-emphasizing churches make. It is nauseating to genuine souls, but not to those who are only interested in outward show—which is the interest of most folk in our churches today.

"If we gain numbers at the expense of spirituality, we do this also at the expense of Divine aid. Better be few, and constituting such a worthy temple that the Holy Ghost can dwell and work in us, than numerous, but possessed by a worldly spirit which degrades the temple into a house of merchandise" (W. F. Adeney). As another has said, "The great want of the church is not more members but more of the right stamp" (T. Kelly). Xerxes discovered that his vast numbers of Asiatic hordes were actually a hindrance to him in warfare against the fewer in number but highly disciplined Greeks. Many a pastor has discovered a similar situation; the large numbers of his church are often a hindrance to a true work of God.

All of this does not discredit every large church. A few got that way by a genuine work of God. But most large churches in so-called fundamental circles in our day have gotten that way by Madison Avenue promotional schemes which put a premium on numbers (which could be boasted about) but not on spirituality. This carnal growth has all been cloaked in evangelism, which makes it difficult to expose. Speak out against these large works and you will be labeled unevangelistic, and your small numbers will be held up in ridicule. But truth is truth; and the day is coming—and some are seeing it already—when the number craze in our churches of the last three or four decades will be found to have been more of a curse than a blessing to the true cause of the spreading of the Gospel of Jesus Christ. We have our thirty-two thousand today, but we are certainly not battling and defeating the Midianites of evil with much success. Instead of another Sunday School contest or pack-the-pew Sunday, our churches need a backdoor revival that would rid its ranks of its worldly members and reduce its numbers to a humble size so God could begin to use the church to do a work for Him.

VI.

Reassurance

Judges 7:9–15

Joseph Parker rightly said, "Gideon was one of those men who require continual encouragement." But we should be careful about being critical of this characteristic of Gideon because of the nature of his duty. He was given a task to do which would overwhelm the best of men. He was placed in circumstances which seemed impossible to conquer. In such a situation we must remember the best of men are still men at their best; and, therefore, they need repeated assurances of their calling and renewed assurances of their success to encourage them to fulfill their duty.

We all will need much encouragement if we have any aspirations about fulfilling the responsibilities of our calling. Any calling of God will experience the opposition of evil which, apart from Divine encouragement, will cause us to give up and retreat from our duties. If you do not sense any need for continual help to keep going, it just may be that you are not trying to do much for the Lord. Marcus Dods said, "That man must have low aims indeed who never finds himself confronted by duty that he feels to be impossible, who does not feel again and again that the conquest of sin in himself is impossible; who is not again and again perplexed by the difficult circumstances he is silently swept into; who does not feel helpless before the profound, rooted misery, the masses of distress and crime in the world." Yes, it is those who are attempting great things for God who sense the greatness of the difficulties and who, therefore, need continual encouragement to keep going.

REASSURANCE

So it was with Gideon in our text. The time had come when he and his small band of three hundred soldiers were to attack the Midianite hordes. Three hundred against one hundred thirty-five thousand was an overwhelming situation; it was a gigantic challenge. Humanly speaking it looked impossible, and it even seemed suicidal to attempt the attack. But just before the attack took place, God stepped in and again encouraged Gideon by giving him reassurance of his calling and of his victory over Midian.

We will note in this chapter the proffer, place, and product of the reassurance God gave Gideon.

A. THE PROFFER OF REASSURANCE

"The LORD said unto him, Arise, get thee down unto the host; for I have delivered it into thine hand. But if thou fear to go down, go thou with Phurah thy servant down to the host: And thou shalt hear what they say; and afterward shall thine hands be strengthened to go down unto the host" (vv. 9,10). This text is often misunderstood. But Keil properly explains it when he says, "The meaning . . . is not, If thou art afraid to go down into the camp of the enemy alone . . . take Phurah . . . with thee . . . The meaning is rather this: Go with thy 300 men into the hostile camp to smite it . . . but if thou art afraid to do this, go down with thine attendant [Phurah] to the camp, to ascertain the state and feeling of the foe, and thou wilt hear what they say." Gideon's orders to begin the attack included an option for reassurance. If he feared to begin the attack, he could then take his servant Phurah and do a bit of reconnaissance of the Midianites. This would result in his hearing talk that would give him reassurance of his calling and of his victory over the Midianites and, thus, encourage him to pursue the attack as God had ordered.

This proffer of reassurance by God was gracious, timely, and accepted.

1. The Proffer was Gracious

The Psalmist said, "As a father pitieth his children, so the

LORD pitieth them that fear him. For he knoweth our frame, he remembereth that we are dust" (Psalm 103:13,14). Gideon had already experienced much encouragement through repeated assurances that he was to deliver Israel from Midian, but God knew Gideon's weaknesses and was ready to give him even more reassurance before he began the actual attack.

God's people can expect Him to give them needed encouragement along the way. True, if God states the promise once, that should be enough. But God often seems desirous of continually encouraging His own by graciously stating the promise repeatedly in order to reassure His own of the truth, of their calling, and of their prospects. So God repeatedly encouraged Gideon by a number of confirmations of his calling. We noted in previous studies that God gave assurances through the visit of the angel of the Lord, through the coming of the Spirit of God upon him, through the response of the people to his call to arms, and through the double sign with the fleece and dew. In this study we see God willing to give him one more assurance of his calling.

This principle of repeated assurances and confirmations is also found in the New Testament regarding the resurrection of Christ. Luke says Christ "shewed himself alive after his passion by many infallible proofs" (Acts 1:3). "Many infallible proofs" manifest the grace of God which encourages us in many, many ways to believe and obey Him. The world does little to encourage us in the right way; but, thankfully, that is not the case with God. God graciously gives us many encouraging assurances if we but listen to Him and observe His working in our lives.

2. The Proffer was Timely

We must note here that this reassurance, which came to Gideon, came at a most opportune time. God knows exactly when we need help and is prompt in providing it. Maclaren said, "How punctually to meet our need, when it begins to be felt, does God's help come." We can count on God to keep us going on the right pathway and to help us to fulfill our responsibilities by giving us the encouraging assurances at just those times when we most need them.

There are two features we need to remember about the timeliness of this encouragement: it comes on the path of obedience, and it seldom comes before it is needed.

First, *it comes on the path of obedience*. Gideon was walking on that path. He had faithfully followed the Lord in every detail. At God's command he had destroyed the altar of Baal, and he had in the hours preceding the attack on Midian reduced the army from 32,000 to a mere 300. Now he had the army in readiness to attack. There was no delinquency here on Gideon's part. He had obeyed well even when obedience was difficult. So when the proffer of encouraging reassurance came, Gideon was most conspicuously on the path of obedience. Those who obey like that can count on God providing them with needed encouragement. But those who are unfaithful will lack the assurances that build confidence and give inspiration for duty.

Second, *it seldom comes before it is needed*. Gideon did not get this present inspiring reassurance until his army had been reduced from 32,000 to only 300 and it was the very moment when he was to send that small group of 300 against the Midianite multitude of 135,000. Sometimes we would like God to give us reassurances long before the need is present. But God prefers we focus our eyes upon Him rather than upon some stockpile of supplies. He will not be tardy in providing needed encouragement, but it frequently does not come until we are at the point where we really need it.

3. The Proffer was Accepted

Gideon had not asked for another sign when God offered him this present reassurance. The fleece sign was the last sign Gideon requested on his own. However, when God gave him an opportunity to obtain more assurance, Gideon did not turn it down. Because of the greatness of his task, Gideon did not spurn an opportunity to have his faith "strengthened" for the task of warring against the Midianites. He jumped at the chance to be reassured that deliverance was indeed going to be his. We believe it was commendable of him here to pursue the reassurance. It indicated that he wanted to face the battle with his faith as strong as possible.

God gives all of us many opportunities to strengthen our faith, to gain more assurance of our beliefs and calling. Today, in our land, we have all sorts of Bible study helps available plus regular opportunities to attend church or hear the Word on radio, etc. But, unlike Gideon, we do not seem very interested in strengthening our faith. Gideon, in seeking more assurance, acknowledged his need of it. God had said, "if thou fear" he could go to the camp of Midian and get more assurance. But we are not about to acknowledge or even recognize our need. Our actions indicate that we seem to think that we are strong enough to face the foe and, therefore, can get along without more spiritual power. Such an attitude will not rout many Midianites, however. It will not move you to attack the Midianites of your soul. Victory over the Midianites only comes when you avail yourself of every opportunity to increase the strength of your faith. You can never be too strong for the foe.

B. THE PLACE OF REASSURANCE

If Gideon wanted reassurance of his calling and thus encouragement to do his duty, he was to take his servant (taking one's servant on a journey or task of any sort was most common in those days) and "go . . . down to the host" of the Midianites. This place of reassurance was a place of opposition, a place of providence, and a place of learning.

1. It was a Place of Opposition

"Go . . . down to the host [Midianites]: And thou shalt hear what they say; and afterward shall thine hands be strengthened" (vv. 10,11). Gideon was to find encouragement in the camp of his enemies, not in the camp of his friends. His reassurance was going to come from the talk of Midianites, not from the talk of Israelites.

Seldom does one expect to receive encouragement from what our adversary says. But when God is directing the scene, we will discover He can give us help from the most unlikely of sources. We do not need the sun to encourage us, for the clouds can do it too—if God so wills it. We do not need good times to give us reassurance that God is caring for us; God can cause even bad times to remind us plainly that He cares for us. In fact, sometimes it is the storm more than the calm that reassures us of God's nearness and help. God will often put us in places of affliction so our faith will grow. Did not the Psalmist say, "It is good for me that I have been afflicted; that I might learn thy statutes" (Psalm 119:71)? The very circumstance with which Satan hopes to overthrow our faith is often that which God uses to build up our faith. Therefore, we are not wise to greatly despair over our difficulties and trials, for they may embody great encouragement for us.

2. It was a Place of Providence

Divine providence is very evident in this experience of Gideon. How often we see in Scripture the dovetailing of events especially for those who are endeavoring to walk according to God's way. Gideon and his servant Phurah came stealthily into the outer edge of the camp of Midian during the darkness of the night. Just as they came near one tent, they heard two Midianites talking. One Midianite man was telling another about a dream he recently had. He said, "Behold, I dreamed a dream, and, lo, a cake of barley bread tumbled into the host of Midian, and came unto a tent, and smote it that it fell, and overturned it, that the tent lay along [flat]. And his fellow answered and said, This is nothing else save the sword of Gideon, the son of Joash, a man of Israel: for into his hand hath God delivered Midian, and all the host" (vv. 13,14).

What wonderful providence to arrive at that tent just as a Midianite was telling another about his dream which had to do with Gideon and the defeat of the Midianites! That the man should at that time tell his dream, that the other man should so quickly and accurately interpret the dream, that they, in spite of the night and the need for caution under the circumstances, should so freely talk so Gideon and Phurah could overhear what they were saying can only be explained as the wonderful providence of God which works marvelously on behalf of those who fear Him.

In the New Testament Paul encourages the faithful by saying, "We know that all things work together for good to them that love God, to them who are the called according to his purpose" (Romans 8:28). This is not a blanket promise for everyone. It is only for those "who love God" and "who are the called according to his purpose [who are abiding in His will]." Such folk will witness many providential circumstances which will reassure and encourage them in their service for the Lord. For those who are walking obediently, providence will confirm the will of God again and again. To the natural eye these providential events may appear insignificant; but to those living according to the plan and purpose of God, it will be a far different story. They will see in the dovetailing of circumstances much which will give assurance of their calling and which will encourage them on God's pathway.

3. It was a Place of Learning

The place of reassurance is always the place of learning. Ignorance does not produce assurance—it might produce false assurance, but we are talking here about genuine assurance. When the two Midianites spoke to each other in the hearing of Gideon and his servant, they gave Gideon considerable knowledge regarding the situation he faced with the Midianite warriors—a knowledge which produced much reassurance of his calling to deliver Israel from the Midianite hordes. Gideon learned at least three important things from these Midianites which gave him reassurance. He learned of the force of weakness, of the fear of Midian, and of the fame of himself.

Reassurance

The force of weakness. The Midianite's dream was about a cake of barley bread tumbling into the camp of Midian and knocking flat a Midianite tent. This work of the barley bread knocking a tent flat is a picture of that which is weak and despised destroying that which, in contrast, is strong and esteemed. Examining both the barley bread and the tent which was knocked flat will emphasize the lesson of the force of weakness—a lesson which God teaches us throughout the Scripture. It is a lesson which says that when we yield ourselves to God to do His will He will make us strong though we be in ourselves very weak.

First, we examine the *barley bread.* A biscuit ("cake" means round, thin, biscuit size) knocking down a tent certainly pictures the force of weakness. Furthermore, what the barley bread represented also emphasized the force of weakness. Barley bread in itself represented the weak and despised. "Barley was usually the food of the poor, and of beasts" (Jamieson). "Such . . . could hardly be eaten by men, it was so vile; a term expressive of the contempt of the Midianites for the people of Israel" (F. C. Cook). This cake of barley bread, as the Midianite interpreter indicated, pictured Gideon. And how accurate the picture, for his "family is poor in Manassah," and he, "the least in my father's house" (Judges 6:15). Yet, in spite of his lack, in spite of his weakness in the eye of man, he is predicted as the one to overthrow the Midianites.

Second, we examine the *tent.* This tent was not a tent of an ordinary person, but it was of either the general of the Midianite army or of the kings of Midian (Midian had two kings, cp. Judges 8:5). Keil says, "'*The tent,*' with the definite article, is probably the principle tent in the camp, i.e. the tent of the general." F. C. Cook says the tent flattened by the barley bread was, "The tent of the king of Midian, or of the captain of the host." Edersheim speaks similarly of the tent when he says the tent was "the principle one, that of the general." Knocking down the tent of the leader would be much more significant than knocking down the tent of an ordinary Midianite, for it would indicate the overthrow of all the Midianites. So knowing what tent was knocked down only emphasizes the lesson on the force of weakness. Weakness overcame the strongest.

This lesson had to give reassurance and thus encouragement to Gideon for his calling. The dream portrayed his situation—poor, weak, and totally unlikely to accomplish what the barley bread did—yet it promised great, even miraculous accomplishment. It reminded and encouraged Gideon that God can work through the weakest of men if they are but surrendered to Him. It reassured Gideon that though he only had 300 soldiers in his army, yet he could deliver a KO punch to Midian with all their 135,000 soldiers. And it reminds us of what Paul said to the believers at Philippi, "I can do all things through Christ, which strengtheneth me" (Philippians 4:13) and of what God said to Paul, "My strength is made perfect in weakness" (II Corinthians 12:9). Paul learned this lesson so well that he said, "Most gladly therefore will I rather glory in my infirmities, that the power of Christ may rest upon me" (Ibid.). It is not our lack of strength that hinders God working in us, rather it is our lack of submission to His will.

The fear of Midian. A second thing Gideon learned, and doubtless much to his surprise, was that Midian was in fear of Gideon and his army. The whole tenor of the dream and its interpretation denotes great apprehension by the Midianites of Gideon and his army. "For into his hand hath God delivered Midian, and all the host" (v. 14), said the Midianite who was interpreting the dream. After seeing a great deal of fear on Israel's side, so much fear in fact that 22,000 of the 32,000 men of Gideon's army went home because their fear was so great, it must have been a great encouragement for Gideon to learn that Midian had fear, too.

Such fear was certainly the work of God in the Midianite hearts, for they could not have been caused to fear by what they saw. The Midianites were "like grasshoppers for multitude; and their camels were without number, as the sand by the sea side for multitude" (v. 12). Such was definitely not the case with the Israelites, however. But the God Who would later cause the Syrian army to "hear a noise of chariots, and a noise of horses, even the noise of a great host" (II Kings 7:6) so that they would cease their siege on Samaria, would have no trouble causing the Midianites to fear even though outward circumstances would not give them reason to fear their destruction.

When we are following the leading of the Lord, as Gideon was, we too will experience this working of God in the hearts of those around us. God will, when necessary, cause people around us to think, act, and speak in most unlikely ways in order to promote and encourage our God-directed work.

The fame of himself. Another thing Gideon learned in this bit of reconnaissance of the Midianites was that he was well known and also well respected by the Midianite soldiers. This would surely also be a great surprise to Gideon. "Gideon the son of Joash, a man of Israel" (v. 14) was the interpreter's statement about Gideon. This said he knew who Gideon was—"the son of Joash," and had great respect for him—"a man of Israel," which means "a mighty or distinguished man of Israel" (Jamieson). Gideon had trouble viewing himself as anything, but now he learns that God has elevated him in the eyes of the Midianites until they have high accolades for him. Spurgeon said, "Gideon must have been awe-stricken when he heard his own name mentioned, and his own success foretold." Awe-stricken, surprised or not, what he heard had to certainly be reassuring to Gideon; and it would greatly encourage the pursuit of his work of attacking Midian.

There is an important lesson here about status, prestige, reputation, fame, and the like. So many people are foolishly spending much of their time tooting their own horn. They often have a very organized campaign to elevate themselves in the eyes of men so they will be respected, given opportunity, honored, and selected for or elected to high position. But how vain and foolish for God's people to be involved in that sort of thing. If God wants us to be esteemed by men, if esteem is necessary in order for us to accomplish our calling, then God will see to it that we will have it—and we will not have to brag on ourselves to get it! Our job is to surrender to the will of God and let God take care of all the rest—the reputation, opportunity, position, etc. The feverish activity of the flesh to push one's self into the spotlight and to pull strings to get the accolades and acceptance of men has nothing whatever to do with faith. If we need reputation, status, prestige, opportunity, or whatever, God can provide it and abundantly.

C. THE PRODUCT OF REASSURANCE

Here we note the difference between faith and unbelief. When unbelief is given signs, it only despises them. But when faith is given signs, it is inspired and encouraged anew to honor and serve God. Gideon's reaction to the reassurance he got in the Midianite camp manifested that he was indeed a man of faith. He did not despise the assurance, the confirmations, and the ratifications God gave him; but he was a good steward of these blessings of God. He used the reassurance here to move him to honor and serve God with new vigor and vitality. For "when Gideon heard the telling of the dream, and the interpretation thereof . . . he worshipped, and returned into the host of Israel, and said, Arise; for the LORD hath delivered into your hand the host of Midian" (v. 15).

The product of this reassuring experience for Gideon was twofold: he worshipped and he warred.

1. He Worshipped

"When Gideon heard the telling of the dream, and the interpretation thereof . . . he worshipped" (v. 15). What a noble product of reassurance. In fact, it is and should be the first result of any assurance. When our faith is strengthened it will show first of all in our worship of God. There is no such thing as an increase in faith that does not manifest itself in an increase in worship.

Reassurance

Many may believe that the reassurance was only necessary for the warring business. But worshipping and warring are inseparably related. We must worship well or we will not serve well. We learned in earlier studies that before Israel could war well against Midian, they had to correct their worship—stop the worship of Baal and revive the worship of Jehovah. The same principle holds true with Gideon. The purpose of the reassurance was to get Gideon to do his duty well, namely, the warring against Midian. But if he is going to war well, he must worship well. Therefore, we should not be surprised to see one of the products of this reassurance being worship. If reassurance is to move Gideon to service, it will also move him to worship—and it did.

The knowledge of this truth—that we must worship well before we serve well—will help guide us in who we ask to teach or put in office at church. We have heard all too often the statement, "Give them a job so they will be more faithful in attendance" as the basis for asking someone to teach a class or for electing someone to a church office. But that philosophy will not find sympathy from Scripture. If one does not worship well he will not serve well. Before we put anyone in a place of service at church, we need to check on their worship habits. Poor attendance habits at church services will reveal poor worship habits and should disqualify from service. The principle is "Let these also first be proved" (I Timothy 3:10) before they are given work to do.

2. He Warred

After Gideon worshipped, he went about the business of warring against the Midianites. He "returned into the host of Israel, and said, Arise; for the Lord hath delivered into your hand the host of Midian" (v. 15). God was strengthening Gideon for his assigned duty by this reassurance. He was not simply filling Gideon's head with curious and interesting facts and figures so Gideon could amuse himself thereby. God had called him to lead Israel against Midian, and the reassurance—coming from the knowledge of what the Midianites were saying and thinking—was given to encourage Gideon to do this work.

When God gives us increased understanding and illumination of the Word of God and when our faith is given more assurance, it is all done to aid and inspire our service. A. F. Muir said, "Do not allow God's gracious revelations in our lives to be a dead letter. Act upon them, that our lives may be brought in subjection and harmony with his will." However, many, who seem quite ready to boast of how they are growing in the knowledge of the Word of God and how their faith is increasing through this increased knowledge, are not evidencing their claims by better service. Their lack in service reveals the phoniness of their claims. Revelation is given for practical application to our lives. Gideon was given knowledge about the Midianites so he would serve better. Believers were instructed about things to come so that "Seeing then that all these things shall be dissolved, what manner of persons ought ye to be in all holy conversation [conduct] and godliness" (II Peter 3:11). Be a good steward of these blessings which encourage faith, and you will serve Him better.

VII.
ROUT

JUDGES 7:16–22

FOR SEVEN LONG years the Midianites assaulted and insulted the Israelites. Each year at harvest time the Midianites moved their hordes into the land and arrogantly plundered the harvest and terrorized the inhabitants. No one dared to lift a hand against them. They seemed invulnerable and undefeatable. But that situation came to a very sudden and convincing end. It came about through the leadership of Gideon, a farmer whom God raised up to be Israel's deliverer. With a small but dedicated group of three hundred soldiers and with a most unique plan of attack, Gideon defeated the Midianites quickly and overwhelmingly. It was a rout of major proportions. So great, in fact, was the defeat of the Midianites that they are never again recorded in Scripture as being enemies of Israel.

In this chapter we are going to take a detailed look at the routing of the Midianites by Gideon and his army which brought an end to the cruel oppression of the Israelites by the Midianites. We will consider the strategy for the rout and the specifics of the rout.

A. THE STRATEGY FOR THE ROUT

To rout the Midianites, Gideon led his three hundred men in one of the cleverest and, in some ways, the strangest attack ever executed by a military group. A. F. Muir says, "The strategy of Gideon is one of the military marvels of antiquity." Gideon's strategy involved the maneuvering for the attack, the munitions for the attack, the mandate for the attack, the moment of the attack, and the manner of the attack.

1. The Maneuvering for the Attack

Upon returning from his bit of spying on the Midianites, in which he heard the telling of the dream that greatly inspired him, Gideon immediately "divided the three hundred men into three companies" (v. 16). This was done so they could be stationed on the hills "on every side of all the camp" (v. 18) and, therefore, "round about the camp" (v. 21) of the Midianites. This was a smart move; for when the attack began, the Midianites would conclude that they were surrounded by the Israelites. This would cause the Midianites greater consternation than if they only perceived the attack was from one direction. Also, being located on the hills surrounding the Midianites ("The host of Midian was beneath him in the valley" [Judges 7:8]), Gideon had an additional advantage in surrounding the Midianites, which the Midianites would not miss; namely, it is much easier to attack your opponent from a hill than from a valley. This, too, would work against the Midianites' spirit once the attack commenced.

Though the stationing of the three groups permitted the Israelites to surround the Midianites, there was, however, an exit left for the Midianites to flee towards their homeland. An opening on the eastern area of the valley, where hills were not blocking their path, was present so the fleeing hordes of Midianites would be able to retreat back towards their land. The three groups of Gideon's army would thus be generally on the south, west, and north side of the Midianite camp.

The location of the troops was very important in this attack, as is true in any attack. Each soldier in Gideon's army must locate himself in the area he was assigned by Gideon if the attack was going to be successful. A soldier may not wish to go to the place he was assigned; but if the attack was to be carried out effectively, each soldier must be in his proper position regardless of his own personal wishes. Christian service is no different. We all have a place assigned to us by the Lord. We may not necessarily like the place we are assigned; but like it or not, we must not question it, for there is a Divine design in the assigning of God's servants. When each is in his proper place, it will cause the work to function most effectively.

One wonders today, when observing the composition of our churches, just how many folk are out of place. We see shortages of workers in one church and an abundance of workers in another church—sometimes so many workers that the church has to rotate them in their duties or leave them to sit and do little. As an example, some churches will have a dozen or so piano players while others will be hard pressed to come up with one decent piano player for their services. Such poor placement of personnel cannot be blamed on God. The problem lies at the feet of God's people. To correct the problem, Christians need to get in tune with God and listen to where He is sending them. Some gravitate to the big churches because there is more prestige in performing before a large crowd than before a small crowd. But we had better let something besides the size of a church determine our location. We had better let God decide where we are to be if we are going to be of use for Him.

2. The Munitions for the Attack

Gideon equipped his soldiers for the battle but with very strange equipment. "He put a trumpet in every man's hand, with empty pitchers, and lamps within the pitchers" (v. 16). The trumpet is better known to us today as the shofar (also spelled shophar). It is generally made of a ram's horn. Today we generally think of the trumpet as being a musical instrument. But in ancient Israel, the trumpet, though used some for music (cp. Psalm 150:3), was chiefly used to herald an announcement or an occasion. The priests used it to signal various special holy days and feasts, and it was used much in regard to war—to call men to battle, to announce an attack, to announce the end of the war, the outcome of the war, etc. Jews still blow it in synagogues and temples today especially on their New Year, Yom Kippur, and on the Day of Atonement. The pitcher was a jug used "for drawing water . . . They were doubtless of earthenware, as they were so easily broken" (A. C. Hervey). The lamps were torches. Wiseman said they were "a flambeau [a flaming torch] of some kind, made probably of resinous wood, and covered with some pitchy substance." The torches were put in the pitchers so they would not be seen by the Midianites when the Israelite soldiers moved around the hills to surround the Midianite camp. To keep the torch from being extinguished in the pitcher, the pitchers had to be of good size and with a large enough opening to provide for adequate oxygen for the torch's fire.

To the natural man this equipment would seem totally inadequate for the task of routing the Midianites. G. A. Rogers said, "Never did means appear more contemptible than those employed by Gideon." But Paul said, "God hath chosen the foolish things of the world to confound the wise; and God hath chosen the weak things of the world to confound the things which are mighty; And base things of the world, and things which are despised, hath God chosen, yea, and things which are not, to bring to nought things that are" (I Corinthians 1:27,28). Why does God choose weapons which are weak and base in the thinking of the wisdom of this world? Paul answered that question in the next verse when he said, "That no flesh should glory in his presence" (I Corinthians 1:29). Gideon's army had been reduced to a mere three hundred in order for God to get the glory; now it is given weaponry which will further contribute to the glory of God.

The early church demonstrated well this truth of God using that which was weak and despised in the eyes of the world to do His work. Unarmed men, despised by the governments of the world and operating under the greatest of disadvantages, swiftly and effectively carried the Gospel to many men and nations. The early church, like Gideon's army, lacked much which we esteem and think necessary today. But, like Gideon's army, they did not lack the power of God—something, unfortunately, we do not seem very interested in at all. We seem more interested in weaponry which is impressive to the flesh and the world. But it is not the weaponry that matters as much as it is the power of God. Obtaining the power of God requires character, however, which is one reason why our day has so little power and plays down its importance.

3. The Mandate for the Attack

The groups were sent to their posts with an important order from Gideon. Gideon, who remained with one of the groups (v. 19), commanded the groups to "Look on me, and do likewise: and, behold, when I come to the outside of the camp, it shall be that, as I do, so shall ye do" (v. 17). Though it was dark and some of the soldiers would be a considerable distance from Gideon, they would have no trouble seeing or hearing what Gideon was doing, which he wanted them to do. The blowing of the trumpet, the breaking of the pitcher, and the displaying of the torch—the things Gideon did which they were to do, which we will note later—could be easily communicated to the troops in the dark and from a distance.

The important thing here is that the soldiers were to follow Gideon's example. What he did they were to do if they were going to rout the enemy. In this we see two important lessons. One lesson concerns Christ as an example and the other lesson concerns Christians as an example.

Christ as an example. Gideon, as the soldiers' captain, ordered them to do as he did, to look upon him as their example. We, who follow the Lord Jesus Christ as the Captain of our souls, have a similar situation with our Lord. He is our example and we are to do as He does. Peter gives an illustration of this truth when he says, "For even hereunto were ye called: because Christ also suffered for us, leaving us an example, that ye should follow his steps" (I Peter 2:21). It is not surprising that Peter referred to Christ as our example, for he would not forget the experience in the upper room which he had with Christ about the washing of his feet which ended with Christ exhorting the disciple, "I have given you an example, that ye should do as

I have done to you" (John 13:15). Yes, Christ has given us example after example of how we should act, and we will never go wrong in following His example. Our problem today is that we are following the wrong examples. We have made wicked worldlings the pattern for our conduct instead of making Christ the example. These heroes of the world, whom we try to emulate, live trashy lives morally, are greedy money grubbers, have profane mouths, and mock Biblical values. We will certainly not defeat any enemy when we make such folk our examples.

Christians as an example. Gideon not only represents Christ, the Captain of our souls, as the example we are to follow; but he also represents what every believer should be to others. As Gideon was an example to his fellow man on how to act in order to have victory in life, so should we be an example to our fellow man. Thus, Paul instructed Timothy to "be thou an example of the believers" (I Timothy 4:12), and exhorted Titus to be "In all things . . . a pattern of good works" (Titus 2:7). Too many professing Christians, however, are an example of disobedience. They only show us how not to act. We need to do some real soul searching to see if our lives are examples of how one should live or of how one should not live. Can we say as Paul said, "Be ye followers of me, even as I also am of Christ" (I Corinthians 11:1)?

4. The Moment of the Attack

The timing of the attack was most opportune. It came "in the beginning of the middle watch; and [when] they had but newly set the watch" (v. 19). This was a most wise move by Gideon for two reasons: it was a time of darkness and a time of distraction.

It was a time of darkness. The middle watch was in the middle of the night. According to Keil and Jamieson, it began at midnight. To attack at this time, in the dead of the night, gave the attackers the advantage of darkness, an advantage which is still respected in military strategy. Attacking at night would keep the Midianites from discovering the smallness of Gideon's army; it would, unlike a daylight attack, add great terror which was vital for the effectiveness of this attack; it would give the attack the element of surprise, which a daylight attack would not do; and it would promote confusion and lack of discernment in the Midianite camp, and thus help the Midianites to unwittingly kill one another, which would encourage the rout.

Since Gideon's attack is indeed the judgment of God upon evil, we have a striking example here of the peril of walking in the darkness of sin. Those who walk in such darkness are unprepared for Divine judgment. It will come upon them "unawares." This is what Christ warned us about in Luke 21:34. "And take heed to yourselves, lest at any time your hearts be overcharged with surfeiting, and drunkenness, and cares of this life, and so that day [judgment] come upon you unawares." We cannot live in sin and be ready for Divine judgment. If you persist in rebellion against God, one day Divine judgment, like Gideon's surprise attack on the Midianites, will come upon you swiftly and forcefully; and you will "suddenly be destroyed, and that without remedy" (Proverbs 29:1).

It was a time of distraction. The attack coming when the watch was "but newly set" meant it came when the quality of the watch was at its poorest. Any military man should know by experience, if not by instruction, that the changing of the watch is a most vulnerable time. The transition from one watch to another causes temporary distraction from surveillance of the watch. With one watch ceasing his vigilance and the other just beginning, the quality of the watch during this transitional time will always be poorer than at other times. Thus near the time of the changing of the guard is a most opportune time to attack, for those attacked are not on their best guard at that time. They are not as alert and discerning, and they are more prone to confusion than at any other time during the watch.

There is a lesson here from this distraction problem which

reminds God's people that they must be ever so careful about letting down their guard. We are glad the Midianites were vulnerable at watch time and that Gideon attacked then. But evil also knows that is a good time to attack; and whenever God's people let down their guard, look out, for evil will strike. We must be ever so vigilant in our watch against evil, or we become vulnerable to spiritual harm.

The moment of attack indicated that Gideon was a very good steward of his circumstances, though they were limited. He had only a very small army, but he still had the opportunity to attack at a very advantageous time. We are to be good stewards of the circumstances and situations God gives us, even if they do seem to be limited. God limited Gideon to a very small army, but Gideon made the best of it by attacking at a very opportune time. A small army attacking at an opportune time can accomplish more than a big army attacking at an inopportune time.

Too often, instead of using what advantages and opportunities we do have, we sit down and pout and fuss about what we do not have. Gideon could have done a lot of complaining about his situation. He could have complained about not having a competitive sized army to face Midian and about not being well armed. But he did not complain. Rather, he busied himself using what advantages he did have and, as a result, accomplished more than anyone would have predicted. We can indeed accomplish much more than we may think if we will only stop complaining of what we do not have and start using wisely what we do have, though what we do have does not seem like much. If you have little money, spend your time budgeting it well rather than complaining about your lack, and you will be pleasantly surprised how much you can do with your small income. If you have few talents to serve in the church, spend your time developing to the fullest those talents, rather than bemoaning your lack of ability to serve, and you will find yourself involved in much rewarding service. If your ministry only seems to reach a few folk, make sure you reach them with a quality ministry rather than lamenting your limited outreach, and you will reach a lot more people than you realize. If you are limited in about everything but time, stop complaining and try to use your time as effectively as possible, and you will do much more than you ever expected. God does not expect us to be a steward of what we do not have; He only expects us to take care of what we do have.

5. The Manner of the Attack

The manner of attack certainly involved some extremely unusual tactics to produce the routing of the Midianites. Though Scripture does not explicitly state that Gideon was instructed by God regarding this attack, it is obvious that God must have communicated the plan to him; for this was not a plan man would devise. Furthermore, if man could devise it, he should not pursue it unless God sanctions the plan. We do not have a license to forsake the normal and common to pursue an extremely unusual way unless God plainly directs us to do so. To pursue, on our own, a plan as unusual as this one and expect God to bless it is not an act of faith but an act of foolishness.

The manner of attack had five aspects to it: the sounding of the trumpets, the smashing of the pitchers, the shining of the torches, the shouting of the battle cry, and the standing of the troops.

The sounding of the trumpets. There was some precedence to this aspect of the attack, but it was still unusual. Going to battle with the sound of trumpets was introduced in Israel early in their history when God said to Moses, "If ye go to war in your land against the enemy that oppresseth you, then ye shall blow an alarm with the trumpets; and ye shall be remembered before the LORD your God, and ye shall be saved from your enemies" (Numbers 10:9). However, this instruction given to Moses did not employ three hundred trumpets; it employed only two (Numbers 10:2). Also, this instruction given Moses did not involve the constant blowing of the trumpets during the attack as was the case in Gideon's attack. Gideon's men did more than just blow the trumpet at the start, they continued to blow the trumpet as they stood on the hills surrounding the Midianites.

While this sounding forth of so many trumpets at one time was not the normal procedure in battle, it was, however, very effective. The sudden blaring forth of the trumpets sounding an alarm in the middle of the night quickly awoke the Midianites and helped cause the fear which contributed so much to the routing of the Midianites.

The blowing of the trumpets took great courage. Nothing they did in that initial attack would take greater courage. To blow a war alarm on those trumpets and to blow it repeatedly would not permit a timid lip, for the sound of the trumpet was the most obvious declaration of war of all the action they took that night on the hills; and it would irretrievably commit them to the battle. Once they blew the trumpet they were committed to the fight. Therefore, it surely was not easy for these soldiers to blast out a war alarm in the middle of the night against an enemy which overwhelmingly outnumbered them.

Those who faithfully preach the Word of God are not altogether in a dissimilar situation as were those trumpeters of Gideon's army. Like Isaiah of old, God would have His preachers "Cry aloud, spare not, lift up thy voice like a trumpet, and show my people their transgression, and the house of Jacob their sins" (Isaiah 58:1). To trumpet a message against sin takes great courage. Once a preacher has trumpeted an attack on evil, he has thrown down the gauntlet. He has plainly positioned himself. People know where he stands and the fight is on.

Unfortunately, we do not have many men in pulpits today who have the courage to trumpet the message of the Word of God against the wickedness of the day. They do not want to get into the fight against evil. So they try to mute the message or even silence it altogether instead of declaring it without apology. They would never be part of Gideon's army, nor will they be part of any victory over evil.

Rout

The smashing of the pitchers. The pitchers in which the torches were concealed were to be broken. When the time came for the attack, the trumpets were to sound then the soldiers were to break the pitchers and hold the lamps in their hands (v. 20). Smashing the pitchers to break them would make a very disconcerting sound to the Midianites. There is always something very upsetting about the sound of breaking glass or pottery (as was done here), and the breaking of as many as three hundred pitchers at one time would really be upsetting, especially at night in these circumstances. That sound, along with the blowing of the trumpets, would certainly awaken, greatly alarm, and contribute much to the routing of the Midianites.

The breaking of the pitchers teaches us some important lessons about service. We would especially emphasize two lessons here. First, the necessity of being broken in order to be of further service; second, the necessity of being totally committed in order to be of further service.

First, the breaking of the pitchers teaches us the necessity of being broken in order to be of further service. The pitchers had a twofold service in this battle against the Midianites. For a short period of time they were to conceal the torches so the enemy would not detect the movement of Gideon's army. When that service was finished, their next assignment was to make a very disconcerting sound to help contribute to the terror and confusion of the Midianites and thus promote the rout. But in order to make the upsetting sound, they had to be smashed to pieces. That seems like waste and loss instead of service. But to be broken here was not waste and loss, for it was indeed necessary to perform important service.

M. R. DeHaan, in his book, *Broken Things*, emphasized the value of broken things when he said, "Before a thing can be made it must be broken. Before the house is built the tree must be broken down. Before the foundation can be laid the rocks must be blasted from their quarry bed where they have long laid in peace and quiet. Before the ripe grain can cover the fields the soil must be broken and beaten small, and the cutting blade of the plow must turn over the sod and the sharp teeth of the harrow pulverize the soil." All of these things were of some service before they were broken; but to be of further service they had to be broken.

Scripture gives a number of examples of the same truth. We note a couple in Christ's ministry. Before a lame man could be healed by Christ, a roof of a house was "broken" up so the man could be placed in the presence of Christ (Mark 2:4), and before Christ fed the multitudes, He "broke" the bread and the fish (Matthew 14:19).

How often we have to be broken to be of further use for God. We may perform some service without being broken, but greater service will be limited if we have not been broken. Frequently the area not broken is our will. Stubborn, self-willed, and unsubmissive, we are not of the use for God we could be if that will was broken.

Second, the breaking of the pitchers teaches us the necessity of being totally committed in order to be of further service. The breaking of the pitchers is a picture of total dedication. Once broken there was no turning back. These pitchers had performed their first service well. But before they could perform further service, they had to be irreversibly committed. So many Christians, however, are not like these pitchers. They never progress in their service for the Lord because they simply are not very committed. They will do some service, but they will never advance far because dedication is deficient. They want to climb a ladder but keep one foot on the ground. They want to jump off the diving board but hang on to the board with one hand. They will never burn their bridges behind them. They will serve if it does not inconvenience them, if it does not interfere too much with their plans. But God is looking for vessels who are irreversibly committed to Him, who are ready to sign up for life, and who will "sell all that thou hast" (Luke 18:22) to serve Him. What is the extent of your commitment to the Lord? How far will you go for Him?

The shining of the torches. Once the torches were taken out of the pitchers, they would really blaze up. All of a sudden the Midianites would be surrounded by some three hundred lights. In the dark of night, this would add to the alarm and panic that would contribute to the routing of the Midianites.

Many commentators see this torch as an example of "Let your light so shine before men, that they may see your good works, and glorify your Father, which is in heaven" (Matthew 5:16). But there is a problem in making that application here. The problem comes about in the fact that there was a time when the light was not supposed to shine. In fact, had it been seen during those times it would have greatly hindered, if not completely stopped, the work of God. Therefore, we need to look for another application; one that better fits the account.

We believe such an application is this: in serving the Lord, times of obscurity are just as important as times of publicity. In our day of high pressured advertisement, gaudy displays, and the constant pushing of self into the spotlight, we may not understand nor appreciate this truth. But we do need to stop being so anxious about being seen and known by man. We should not fret if God sticks us in some pitcher circumstance in which we are hardly known or observed. In such times we must not give up but keep the fire going; for when the time comes, God will thrust us into the public eye. But if we are thrust into the public eye too soon, we may be a bigger problem than a blessing.

John the Baptist, who was "a burning and a shining light" (John 5:35), spent many years in the pitcher of "the deserts till the day of his showing unto Israel" (Luke 1:80). What a mess he would have made of things if he had come out of the deserts before his time to shine had arrived. Interestingly, after John ministered for a short time, he was again taken out of public view. It started when he began to lose his crowd to Christ. This upset his loyal disciples, but John had a good answer for them when he said, "He must increase, but I must decrease" (John 3:30). Any person who would serve the Lord properly must embrace this attitude if their light is to shine at the right places and times.

Jesus Christ also went through the pitcher experience. He "for thirty years, during which He prepared Himself for His short ministry, lived a life of retirement and subjection at Nazareth. In His career on earth there was no precocious self-assertion, no premature display" (H. E. J. Bevan). If even Jesus Christ experienced the seclusion of the pitcher, we surely should not complain if we are thrust into some obscure, unnoticed place for a time. Just remember that regardless of how obscure the situation, be faithful and keep the fire burning in your soul. Someday your time will come when you are to "Arise, shine; for thy light is come, and the glory of the LORD is risen upon thee" (Isaiah 60:1).

The shouting of the battle cry. Gideon instructed the three hundred to shout "The sword of the LORD, and of Gideon" when the signal (which was his blowing of the trumpet [v. 18]) was given to do so. It was not unusual for an army to have a battle cry. Battle cries can be very important; they can state a cause and inspire action. Some famous battle cries, such as— "Remember the Alamo"—have come from our own country's battles.

This battle cry said some important things. I. M. Haldeman said, "That cry recognized the Lord was fighting for them; it recognized that they were fighting in the company with the Lord. It was the declaration that they were co-workers together with God." Luke Wiseman said the battle cry spoke "The two names they [the Midianites] most dreaded, Jehovah and Gideon." It was therefore a battle cry which both Israel and the Midianites needed to hear if Israel was to have victory over the Midianites.

The battle cry initiated by Gideon involved a good deal of commendable humility by Gideon. After he had earlier heard the phrase, "the sword of Gideon" (7:14), spoken by the Midianite who was interpreting the dream of his fellow Midianite, Gideon wisely incorporated the phrase in the battle cry because it would be clearly understood and feared by the Midianite hordes. But he altered it to give the Lord the first place. With him it was first "the sword of the LORD"; then it was the sword of Gideon. Gideon had it straight. He gave credit where credit was due. He wanted the Midianites to know that Jehovah was involved in this victory, not just Gideon; and that Jehovah was the Prime Mover of the attack.

When our battle cries put the Lord in that position, we will be winning more battles. Too often our slogans put the emphasis upon man instead of God. Churches often fail here. As an example, "We care, come and see" is a slogan a number of churches have. It shows up on their stationery, on their outdoor signs, and in their advertisements. But it is not a good slogan because the emphasis is on the church, not Christ.

The standing of the troops. Another interesting, unusual, but wise feature of the manner of attack was that the three hundred troops did not actually charge the camp during the beginning of the rout. "They stood every man in his place round about the camp; and all the host [Midianites] ran, and cried, and fled" (v. 21). Later on, Gideon and these three hundred did indeed pursue the remnants of the Midianites across the Jordan (8:4); but for a time at the outset of the attack they stood firm while the Midianites fled. Their duty at the beginning was simply to blow the trumpet, smash the pitchers, hold up the torches, and shout the battle cry—all while they stood firm in one place.

This action by Gideon and his men was very important. Had they charged down the hill after breaking the pitchers and blowing the trumpets, they would have revealed to the Midianites their movements, their number, and that they had only a trumpet (in their right hand) and torch (in their left hand) to do battle. This would have ended the rout in short order. But standing firm for a time kept the Midianites in great terror and suspense so that the rout gained irreversible momentum.

It is generally much harder to stand still than to be actively moving about, especially in a moment of excitement such as Gideon and his three hundred were experiencing at that time. But God orders our stops as well as our starts. It is not running hither and yon that speaks of dedication, it is obedience. "Company halt!" must be obeyed just as much as "Forward march!" Heeding a stop sign will not hinder your progress, but ignoring it could bring all progress to an abrupt halt. Our Commander knows the situation better than we; and His commands are based on His knowledge which is complete, not on our knowledge which is incomplete.

B. THE SPECIFICS OF THE ROUT

When Gideon and his three hundred troops blew the trumpets, smashed the pitchers, held up the torches, and shouted, "The sword of the LORD and Gideon," the Midianites were quickly routed. They "ran, and cried, and fled . . . and the LORD set every man's sword against his fellow" (vv. 21,22). There are at least three specific characteristics about the Midianites in this rout which are most evident in these verses: the Midianites were fearful, foolish, and fratricidal.

1. They Were Fearful

What fear would suddenly sweep over the camp of the Midianites when the attack began. First, from a nearby hill there was the piercing sound of a trumpet blast which, because of the night hour, would be an eery, nerve chilling sound. This was then quickly followed by the disconcerting sound of pottery being smashed and by the sudden appearance of a torch on top of one of the hills surrounding the camp. Immediately, there came a great increase of this alarming sound and sight from the hills all around the camp as three hundred more trumpets sounded, three hundred more pitchers were smashed, and three hundred more torches lit up the night. Then added to that was the three hundred men shouting the alarming (to the Midianites) battle cry. Terror would permeate the camp of the Midianites. With the blare of trumpets continuing, the battle cry being repeated again and again, and the torches flaring up in the air now that they were out of the pitchers, Gideon and his army simply terrorized the Midianites into flight. The evidence of their great fear is seen in the statement "all the host ran, and cried, and fled."

That the Midianites should be driven from Israel by fear is most fitting. As Matthew Henry said, "It was intended that those who had so long been a terror to Israel, and had so often frightened them [cp. Judges 6:2], should themselves be routed and ruined purely by terror." God often punishes people for their sin in the same coin in which they sinned. The Midianites certainly had this experience. Those who cause unnecessary terror to others will some day be terrorized themselves. We sow and we reap, and we reap what we sow.

2. They Were Foolish

When Gideon's small army commenced their unique attack, the Midianites quickly "fled" the valley of Jezreel; and, in short order, they had "fled to Beth-shittah in Zererath, and to the border of Abel-meholah [later the birthplace of Elisha] unto Tabbath" on their way back to the land of Midian (vv. 21, 22). Their fleeing, while of great benefit to the Israelites, really displayed much folly on the part of the Midianites because no one was chasing them. In fact, as we noted previously, Gideon and his three hundred men were standing still—all they were doing was blowing their trumpets, shouting their battle cry, and holding up their torches. Later on, of course, the Midianites were indeed chased by a host of Israelites; but that was only after the Midianites had fled from the valley of Jezreel and were obviously headed back to their own land. Had they not fled the scene when Gideon and his three hundred soldiers made their presence known, there would have been no chasing of the Midianites by the Israelites. The Israelites only gave chase when they saw the Midianites flee.

The Midianites' folly was to act before they ascertained the facts. They were literally bluffed into a rout. Gideon made a mockery of Midian might by the manner in which he caused them to flee the country. The Midianites became the laughing stock of the ages for fleeing en masse so quickly when no one was pursuing. But God ever makes fools out of those who oppose Him. And one of the ways in which the wicked are made fools is in the fact that "The wicked flee when no man pursueth" (Proverbs 28:1).

Furthermore, God ever makes fools out of those who mistreat the Jews, something the Midianites were certainly doing. Nation after nation that has been a persecutor of the Jews has been brought low and made a fool in the eyes of the world. And how often many of these nations have, like Midian, had military might that far surpassed the military might of the Jews; yet the Jews have won astonishing victories anyway, much to the embarrassment and the shame of the Jew-hating nations.

3. They Were Fratricidal

In the confusion of the situation, the Midianite hordes began killing each other. "The LORD set every man's sword against his fellow, even throughout all the host" (v. 22). It is not difficult to see how the Lord worked this fratricide amongst the Midianites. When they were awakened, their only thought was an attack by the Israelites; and so they expected that Israelite soldiers would be invading the camp swinging their swords in death dealing blows. Being dark (today, with our abundance of artificial lighting, we do not appreciate how dark things are when there are no street lights or other artificial lighting) they could easily mistake those of their own, who were running around waving swords to counter the Israelites, as being Israelites who had invaded the camp. In the dark the Midianites would begin attacking, with a sword or other war implements, any form they could, thinking it was the enemy. Not being able to distinguish friend from foe, they killed each other. This had to be a great contributing factor to the terrible slaughter which occurred among the Midianites; so that before Gideon captured and slew the two kings of Midian, 120,000 of the 135,000 "who drew sword" (Judges 8:10) had already been slain.

God was behind this fratricide, as our text plainly states. Just as God was helping Gideon's group to wage war successfully, so He helped the Midianites to self-destruct. But what a terrible thing it is to have God fighting against you. Yet, that is the experience of so many. They have set themselves against God, and when you set yourself against God, you only set God against yourself.

If you are complaining that it seems God is working against you much of the time, the problem will be found in your own ways which are continually against God. Going against God's will, against God's Word, against God's way in your life will not find God working with and for you; rather He will be working against you. But how much better to submit to God as Gideon did and experience God working wonderfully on your behalf.

VIII.

Rancor

Judges 7:23 – 8:3

REGARDLESS OF HOW great our victory or accomplishment is in God's work, we will seldom be long without experiencing animosity from those who seem to forever exude a sour spirit. These people are habitual critics of that which is good. They always have some complaint, some grievance, some personal slight—real or, as is generally the case, imaginary—which they must air with an indignant spirit; and they will counter every accolade we receive with an accusation.

Gideon was not without this problem. Shortly after the Midianites had been routed and were fleeing back to their wilderness homes east of the Jordan, the tribe of Ephraim confronted Gideon. "And they did chide with him sharply" (8:1) about a personal slight they incorrectly perceived (do these folk ever perceive anything correctly?) Gideon was guilty of, in regards to his treatment of the Ephraimites.

The rancor which the Ephraimites displayed was so out of spirit with the victorious occasion the day was the for Israelites. For seven years the Midianites had tormented the Israelites, but Gideon had led Israel in an astounding rout of these wicked neighbors of Israel and had given Israel freedom again. What a wonderful day this was for God's people! You would think all the Israelites would be celebrating the victory. But in spite of the rout, there was still a dissident element in Israel which, instead of rejoicing in victory, preferred to display itself in rancorous behavior.

In our study of the rancor of the Ephraimites, we will consider the prelude to the rancor, the protest from the rancor, and the placating of the rancor.

A. THE PRELUDE TO THE RANCOR

After the initial routing of the Midianites from the valley of Jezreel, the Midianites were pursued south and east towards the Jordan and across the Jordan back towards their own land. Not only was Gideon and his three hundred involved in this pursuit, but also many other Israelites joined in with Gideon and his faithful few in chasing down and slaying the Midianites. This pursuit was the prelude to the rancor of the Ephraimites. It led to the situation in which the Ephraimites would confront Gideon and vent their uncalled-for anger against him.

We will consider the sagacity of the pursuit, the spontaneity in the pursuit, the solicitation for the pursuit, and the success of the pursuit.

1. The Sagacity of the Pursuit

Napoleon "is said to have maintained that the skill of a consummate general is never so critically tested as in deciding how to turn victory to the best advantage" (Wiseman). Napoleon would have been impressed with Gideon, for Gideon took wise advantage of the initial victory over the Midianites by pursuing these plunderers of Israel until they were so destroyed they were no longer able to cause Israel more trouble. The pursuit secured a complete victory for Israel over the Midianites. In fact, as we noted in our last chapter, the victory was so complete that the Midianites were never again recorded in Scripture as being a problem for Israel.

Another general who would be impressed with Gideon would be General Douglas MacArthur. MacArthur also believed in total victory, and so he would highly approve of Gideon's pursuit of the Midianites until they were destroyed. Unfortunately MacArthur's desire for total victory was not shared by his superiors during the Korean War. As a result, communism maintained a strong foothold in Korea in spite of the war. MacArthur wanted to drop a few small A-bombs in strategic places in Manchuria to eliminate the communist problem in Korea. Had this been permitted, North Korea, as well as South Korea, would have been freed from communist domination. Furthermore, this action probably would have also prevented the Vietnam War. MacArthur, like Gideon, wanted to pursue the enemy all the way back into his own country and destroy him. But he was not allowed by his superiors—the United Nations and Harry Truman—to do this; and so, unlike Gideon's success over the Midianites, MacArthur was not able to subdue the communists in the Korean War.

Thankfully, after the debacles of the Korean and Vietnam Wars, our nation acted much more wisely against Iraq in the Persian Gulf War. The result was a quick and overwhelming victory that brought much destruction upon Iraq and made them unable to be the menace they were before the war. Though Iraq should have been subdued even more than it was, the Desert Storm War did reflect a Gideon-type victory—the only way to wage war against a vicious enemy.

Evil cannot be overcome by gently slapping it on the wrist. It must be dealt with firmly, or we will not subdue it. But tragically, we seldom take that kind of action against evil in our day. Children are spared the rod; criminals are given light sentences though their crimes are atrocious; church dissidents are scarcely dealt with at all; and, in our personal lives, we take very little firm action against our besetting sins. As a result, we do not see much real victory over evil. Like in Korea and Vietnam, we fight no-win wars against evil because we simply will not oppose evil firmly and forcibly.

Jesus gave some choice instruction about dealing firmly with evil, particularly personal sin, when He said, "And if thine eye offend thee, pluck it out: it is better for thee to enter into the kingdom of God with one eye than, having two eyes, to be cast into hell fire" (Mark 9:47). That is drastic action to say the least, but it is also very wise action as the results indicate. If Christians were to follow this principle of Christ in dealing firmly with evil, one of the things many of them should do is throw out their TV set. Drastic action, yes. Too drastic for most. But you cannot argue with the results Christ gave. Nor can you argue with the results Gideon obtained when he wisely pursued the Midianites until complete victory was secured.

2. The Spontaneity in the Pursuit

Here we focus on those who first joined up with Gideon and his three hundred men to pursue the Midianites. After the initial rout, which came when Gideon and his three hundred blew the trumpets, smashed the pitchers, held up the torches, and shouted their battle cry of "the sword of the LORD and of Gideon," others became aware of the fleeing Midianites and quickly and spontaneously set out to pursue them. "And the men of Israel gathered themselves together out of Naphtali, and out of Asher, and out of all Manasseh, and pursued after the Midianites" (7:23). These pursuers were "the men of these tribes whom Gideon had sent away before the battle" (Keil). Not qualified for the special task of starting the rout, they, however, were able to give a hand once the rout commenced and did so enthusiastically without being prodded.

One has to commend these rejects for their willingness to pursue the Midianites even though they had earlier been dismissed from Gideon's army. They could have done like so many in church do—if they cannot serve in one position, they refuse to serve in any position. But though these soldiers were disqualified for the high position of the first attack on the Midianites, they were still willing to help where and when they could.

Many in church, for one reason or another, are not qualified for high office; but there are other tasks they could do, if they would. But, unlike the rejects of Gideon's army, most of these members who are not qualified for high office do not respond very well to the other tasks. They are too small spiritually to keep from getting miffed if they cannot hold some high office. So instead of helping where they could, they go off on a pout and refuse to do anything. Such folk miss many blessings and hinder the work of God much more than they realize. They also, by their refusal to serve in other positions, only vindicate their disqualification from the higher posts. Their unwillingness to serve in humbler positions exposes a character that is definitely not qualified for a higher position.

3. The Solicitation for the Pursuit

"And Gideon sent messengers throughout all mount Ephraim, saying, Come down [the Ephraimites lived in the hill country west of Jordan] against the Midianites, and take before them the waters unto Beth-barah and the Jordan. Then all the men of Ephraim gathered themselves together, and took the waters unto Beth-barah and Jordan" (v. 24). In fleeing back towards their homeland, the Midianites went in a southeasterly direction from the valley of Jezreel in order to cross the Jordan at good crossing places. In following this route, they would also have to cross some streams ("waters") on the west of Jordan just before crossing the Jordan. Gideon, sizing up the situation expertly, sent word ahead to the Ephraimites—who were located south of the valley of Jezreel and, therefore, conveniently in the path of the fleeing Midianites—to take control of the fords of these various streams and of the Jordan which the Midianites would have to cross. Beating the Midianites to these crossings would effectively cut off the fleeing Midianites and enable the Israelites to better destroy them.

The Ephraimites quickly responded. "Then all the men of Ephraim gathered themselves together, and took the waters unto Beth-barah and Jordan" (7:24). There was no hint in their response that they were piqued at Gideon and would shortly contend with him in a very unsavory way. But oftentimes people with sour spirits and unsavory characters do indeed work energetically and give an appearance of support and unanimity in some good project at the beginning. This, to the undiscerning, gives these bad characters an apparent show of credibility and, thus, an undue respect for their contentious ways. However, we must realize that all service, though it may accomplish many good things, does not always commend the characters of the performers. "Some indeed preach Christ even of envy and strife" (Philippians 1:15). All do not preach Christ "of good will" (Ibid.). Therefore, we must not condone a person just because he or she is a famous gospel singer with a great voice, or is a dynamic speaker, or attracts great crowds to his meetings or his church. Check out their character before you accept their person and give respect to their ways.

4. The Success of the Pursuit

Gideon's plan of pursuit worked well. Chased from behind, the Midianites ran into the blockade of the Ephraimites in front of them. Some Midianites, under the leadership of the Midianite kings (Zebah and Zalmunna, cp. Judges 8:10), escaped this blockade by either crossing the Jordan before the blockade was put into effect or by crossing it at more difficult but unblockaded crossings farther up stream. However, in spite of some not being stopped by the blockade, it was still very effective; for a great slaughter of the Midianites took place. The climax of the slaughter by the Ephraimites being the slaying of the "two princes of the Midianites, Oreb and Zeeb . . . they slew Oreb . . . and Zeeb . . . and brought the heads of Oreb and Zeeb to Gideon on the other side of Jordan [Gideon had already crossed Jordan in pursuit of the two kings of Midian]" (7:25).

Such a great slaughter took place in this Gideon-planned confrontation of the Midianites with the Ephraimites that it was celebrated many years later in the Psalms (Psalm 83:9–11) and Isaiah (Isaiah 10:26) along with such deliverances as the Red Sea experience as one of the great examples of God's vengeance upon Israel's enemies. Gideon, when first called by God to deliver Israel, had complained "where be all . . . [the] miracles which our fathers told of, saying, Did not the LORD bring us up from Egypt?" (Judges 6:13). But no longer can he lament the lack of Divine miracles, for that which God did against the Midianites of Gideon's day became one of the great victories memorialized by Israel.

GIDEON

And this victory came about because one man, this very Gideon, gave himself fully to the Lord. Yet, as we will see next, the great dedication and devotion of Gideon was ignored; and he became the subject of heated criticism by a people who, because of their poor attitudes, had lost sight of the great victory and its blessing upon the land.

B. THE PROTEST FROM THE RANCOR

"And the men of Ephraim said unto him [Gideon], Why hast thou served us thus, that thou calledst us not, when thou wentest to fight with the Midianites? And they did chide with him sharply" (8:1). Rancor now mars the scene. Everything was going so well, then the Ephraimites act up and protest to Gideon about how they think they were wrongly treated.

We will consider the communication and the character of the protest.

1. The Communication of the Protest

We want to note two things about the communication of the rancorous protest to Gideon. We will first note when it was communicated, and then we will note who communicated it.

When it was communicated. The protest occurred when God was doing a great work for Israel in delivering them from the Midianites. Particularly, it came at a time when Israel had gained a great victory in one of the key battles with the Midianites. The blockade by the Ephraimites, ordered by Gideon, had just resulted in a great slaughter of the Midianites and was climaxed in the slaying of two chief princes of Midian, Oreb and Zeeb. It was when the Ephraimites triumphantly brought the heads of the two princes to Gideon that the rancorous protest was communicated to Gideon.

The timing of the coming of the protest was not accidental. It was typical. Whenever the Lord does a work, you can count on the devil to quickly try to counter the work. Since God had indeed been doing a great work in destroying the Midianites, we should not be surprised at this rancorous intrusion into the victorious battling against the Midianites. When our ship is sailing well in the spiritual sea, it will not be long before Satan comes along and stirs up the sea to try to hinder our voyage. He will try to disrupt and discourage the work as much as he can. Here in Gideon's case, Satan was not able to do a great deal of harm; but he was able to disrupt the work temporarily. Gideon and his three hundred needed to be on their way in the final campaign to destroy the Midianites and the two Midianite kings. But their progress is unnecessarily slowed while the Ephraimites vent their anger against Gideon. This helped the fleeing Midianites to gain a bit of ground on Gideon—thus requiring Gideon and his already tired crew (cp. Judges 8:4) to expend more energy to catch them.

How often this type of interruption happens to God's servants. As an example, in the midst of a great week of special meetings or when a much needed building program is progressing well, a pastor will have his busy schedule interrupted by a phone call from some sour-spirited Ephraimite full of rancor. Nothing good comes of these time-consuming phone calls, and such calls only hinder the work by disrupting it and by riling the spirit to make it more difficult to do the work. But to be forewarned is to be forearmed. Therefore, to know that these experiences will come, when we are endeavoring to do the Lord's work and are especially enjoying progress in the Lord's work, will help us to be ready for them so they will not have the effect Satan would like them to have upon us.

Who communicated it. This rancorous protest came from the Ephraimites, not from the Midianites. The devil was no longer having any success in opposing the work of God by working through the Midianites; so he switched to working through the Ephraimites. If he cannot be successful in countering the work on one front, he will move to another front. If Satan cannot hinder a work from without, he will try to hinder it from within. And, sad to say, working from within has often proved to be much more effective for the devil than working from without; for the devil does not seem to have much trouble finding disgruntled Ephraimites within God's camp who will become most willing tools of his. Old time preachers tell about the booze and gambling and theater crowd opposing revival meetings in their day. But today the problems in revival meetings are more likely to be sour-spirited church members. The devil does not have to use the booze, gambling, and theater crowd anymore because the church has more than enough Ephraimites in it to do his work. But woe is he who becomes a useful tool for Satan. The day will come when judgment will fall from God, and it will not be pretty. This eventually happened to the Ephraimites some years later, as we will note shortly.

2. The Character of the Protest
The protest which the Ephraimites made to Gideon reeked of bad character. Particularly we will note it was selfish, arrogant, deceptive, and mean.

Selfish. As soon as the Ephraimites opened their mouth, they gave away their selfishness. "Why hast thou served [or treated] us thus" were their first few words. This statement made it very obvious whom they were chiefly concerned about. They were chiefly concerned about how they, the Ephraimites, were served and treated.

When a person is controlled by selfishness, he will judge every situation by how it treats him. But on the other hand, a selfish person demands very little responsibility of himself in treating others properly. So these Ephraimites will not be bothered by their very poor treatment of Gideon in their protesting encounter with him, which mistreatment we will note shortly. What concerns them is how Gideon is treating them.

Society is filled with this selfish spirit of the Ephraimites. Unions reflect it most conspicuously. They are greatly concerned about how much the workers are paid by their employers, but they seem very disinterested in what kind of a job the workers do for their employers. A great many marriage problems have their roots in selfishness, too. Any pastor, or other person, who has counseled those with marriage problems will tell you that each spouse will complain much about how the other spouse has failed to treat them properly but is very reluctant to admit they have not always treated their spouse properly. If marriage partners would be more concerned about how they treated their mates than vice versa, most marriage problems would disappear overnight. Churches also are plagued with problems because of Ephraimite selfishness. Many are the members who are quick to accuse the pastor of not treating them right who never concern themselves about how they treat the pastor. These gripers, who often have a salary two or three or more times larger than the pastor, see to it that the pastor's salary is meager, and that he is expected to work twice as many hours a week to get his salary as they do for their much larger salary. Yet, they complain about the pastor mistreating them! How sick and how selfish. It is the spirit of the Ephraimites which produces such rancorous behavior.

Arrogant. "Thou calledst us not" is the language of an arrogant person who thinks he is more important than he is. They were put out because they were left out of the initial call to arms which Gideon extended shortly after he had torn down the altar of Baal. Gideon had "sent messengers throughout all Manasseh; who also was gathered after him: and he sent messengers unto Asher, and unto Zebulun, and unto Naphtali; and they came up to meet him" (Judges 6:35); but he did not send any messengers to Ephraim. Ephraim did not border the valley of Jezreel as most of these other tribes did, and thus they were not as close to the valley where the Midianites were as the other tribes were who were called by Gideon. Gideon's plan was obviously to first call the tribes who were closest to the Jezreel valley and who were therefore the most affected by the Midianite invaders. Later Gideon did, however, call Ephraim when the Midianites moved into the area near Ephraim. But that was not good enough for them now. They feel they were slighted, and arrogant people get very upset if they think they have been slighted. Not one slight, real or imagined, will escape their notice and loud protest.

Arrogant people are difficult to get along with. They may do their work well at times, as the Ephraimites did in blocking and slaying the fleeing Midianites and in capturing and killing Oreb and Zeeb; but their arrogant attitudes cause them to disturb things, upset relationships, create animosity, and imperil the work. Charles Simeon, in commenting on the Ephraimites, well described the proud man when he said, "See the proud man, swelling with a sense of his own importance: If you differ from him in judgment, or act contrary to his will, yea, if you do not comply with his humour in everything, he is quite indignant, and bursts forth into rage. Even the best-meant endeavors cannot always please him: as an inferior, he cannot brook the least restraint: as a superior, he never thinks that sufficient homage is paid to him: and as an equal, he cannot endure that others should exercise the liberty which he arrogates to himself."

Deceptive. The Ephraimites' complaint implied they would have responded enthusiastically to Gideon's call if he had called them. But that is simply not the case. The Ephraimites were the kind that only responded to the call to arms when a favorable outcome and glory were assured—such as was the case when Gideon called them to block the river crossings. If they were so concerned about driving the Midianites out of the land at first, why did they not volunteer their services when Gideon was calling the other tribes? As Matthew Henry says, "Why did not the Ephraimites offer themselves willingly to the service? They knew the enemy was in their country, and had heard of the forces that were raising to oppose them, to which they ought to have joined themselves in zeal for the common cause, though they had not a formal invitation." Jamieson speaks the same when he says, "Had they been really fired with the flame of patriotic zeal [they would] have volunteered their services in a movement against the common enemy." But when Gideon extended the call the first time, the outcome did not look certain; in fact, it looked very bad for the Israelites.

The real reason the Ephraimites protested was that they were sore they were going to miss out on some glory. There was much glory to be had in leading the first attack on the despised, marauding Midianites. What courage and bravery, and patriotism would be attributed to those who were first to challenge the Midianites. Of course, had Gideon not been so successful, the Ephraimites would not have complained at all, but they would have been very glad they had been excluded from the battle. But now that Gideon has been very successful, they were upset about the glory they would miss because they were not called earlier.

This same deceptiveness in the Ephraimites is seen in a similar incident they had some years later with Jephthah. Then they were indeed called to battle; but, with victory uncertain, they refused to come. However, when the battle turned into a great victory for Israel, they again complained at not being called at first (Judges 12:1–3). We will look at that experience more fully towards the end of this chapter. Suffice it now to simply note that there was considerable deceptiveness in their protest, a deceptiveness which seems to have been most characteristic of the Ephraimites.

This deceptiveness often shows up in the Lord's work even today. Some in our churches, who showed no interest in being involved when a new project or work began—in fact, they often vigorously opposed the endeavor—complain quite loudly about being left out of the work after the work has become a great success. They only became interested in the work after it had proven to be successful, and there was praise being given to those involved. But you would never know it by their protest. The way they whine and complain about being left out, you would think they originated the project.

Mean. "They did chide with [reprimand] him sharply [vigorously, strongly]." These Ephraimites really went after Gideon. Their words were strong, bitter, and cutting. They gave him a very harsh rebuking, though, in fact, he had done nothing wrong. "Gideon had committed no offense at all: he had acted altogether by the direction of God: and so far was he from being at liberty to increase his army by the accession of the Ephraimites, that he was necessitated to reduce the thirty-two thousand troops which he had raised to three hundred" (Charles Simeon). So to reprimand him and so strongly was totally unjustified and therefore very mean. Joseph Parker so despised their conduct that he said, "We almost long for Ephraim to come into contact with the other kind of man [a reference to the severe judgment they experienced from Jephthah when they pulled the same act on him—which judgment we will note more of later]."

Such a confrontation could not be anything but painful to Gideon. It had to hurt. Here was a man who had struggled with the call to take on the Midianite oppressors, who far outnumbered his small forces. Yet, he obeyed and did as commanded by the Lord, and he courageously led the attack against Midian. Then in wise follow-up action, he told the Ephraimites to throw up a blockade in front of the fleeing Midianites by the fords of the waters and streams they must cross. All of this action was very successful. Israel was quickly being delivered from the terrible oppression of the Midianites. But what is Gideon's reward at the moment—a severe dressing down by his own people. How mean were these people! How terribly they mistreated God's servant!

Many preachers can identify with Gideon, for they have many confrontations with this type of people. Oftentimes it seems to happen right after a church service, right after the pastor has labored diligently in preaching the Word of God. Some dear folk show their appreciation for the message by their encouraging comments. But there are always those who, like the mean Ephraimites, will come up to the pastor soon after the sermon and blast away about some alleged problem he is to them. These people do not seem to mind who is listening or how much time they take; they simply have to show their rancor. Such conduct is just plain meanness. It is uncalled for and certainly does nothing to help a preacher or the work of God. But preachers, if they are to succeed and keep going, have to be like Gideon and take the mean confrontation with much grace. Matthew Henry said, "Very great and good men must expect to have their patience tried by the unkindnesses and follies even of those they serve and must not think it strange." Every pastor will have many mean Ephraimites in his congregation. Therefore, he needs to pray daily for grace and skill to deal with them so they do not extinguish his fire and zeal for God and His work.

C. THE PLACATING OF THE RANCOR
"And he [Gideon] said unto them, What have I done now in comparison with you? Is not the gleaning of the grapes of Ephraim better than the vintage of Abiezer? God hath delivered into your hands the princes of Midian, Oreb and Zeeb: and what was I able to do in comparison with you? Then their anger was abated toward him, when he had said that" (8:2,3). Gideon poured oil on the tempest and quieted the rancor of the complaining Ephraimites so he could quickly continue the battle against the Midianites. This placating of the rancor was impressive, incriminating, and impermanent.

1. The Placating was Impressive

Gideon's handling of the rancorous protest was impressive. Charles Simeon was so impressed with Gideon's handling of this problem that he said, "His defeat of all the Midianitish hosts with only three hundred men . . . is less worthy of admiration, than the self-possession he exercised towards the offended and objurgatory Ephraimites." Simeon has good grounds for his statement, for Proverbs 16:32 says, "He that is slow to anger is better than the mighty; and he that ruleth his spirit, [is better] than he that taketh a city." But we are apt to honor military, sports, business, and other secular achievements far more than the achievement of controlling the spirit. This is just another indication of how condemningly different we think than God thinks.

Gideon's restrained response to the Ephraimites' outbursts occurred because he was not concerned about his own glory, as were the Ephraimites. Gideon valued God's glory and the welfare of Israel above his own praise. Therefore, he willingly lowered himself to placate the Ephraimites by saying, "What have I done now in comparison to you?"

Of course, few, if any, would agree that the Ephraimites had done more than Gideon. They certainly had accomplished something in the slaughter of the Midianites and the slaying of Oreb and Zeeb, but Gideon was the great deliverer of Israel. He had spearheaded the attack and was "the mighty man of valor," whom God signally used to drive the Midianites out of the land. But Gideon, in taking a back seat to the Ephraimites, followed a principle penned nearly twelve hundred years later by the Apostle Paul: " . . . in lowliness of mind let each esteem others better than themselves" (Philippians 2:3).

In lowering himself, Gideon was careful, however, not to take anything away from God to placate the Ephraimites. As Matthew Henry said, "Though to magnify their achievements, he is willing to diminish his own performances, yet he will not take any flowers from God's crown to adorn theirs . . . [for he said when praising them] God hath delivered into your hands the princes of Midian."

Yes, we are impressed with the spirit that Gideon exhibited in dealing with the rancorous Ephraimites. It is not easy to deal with such folk. But when one is not concerned about how much glory he does or does not get, it will be much easier for him to deal with the deprecating behavior of others towards him.

2. The Placating was Incriminating

The Ephraimites incriminated themselves by what placated their anger. When Gideon praised them for their capture of Oreb and Zeeb and said, "What was I able to do in comparison with you?" that was enough to silence them. "Then their anger was abated toward him, when he had said that." The one thing the Ephraimites wanted was praise. They were addicted to self-glory. So Gideon did not have to satisfy them with a good explanation as to why the Ephraimites were not called. They did not care about explanations; all they cared about was exaltations. They tried to disguise their glory-seeking under the guise of seeking an explanation; but as soon as they got some exaltation, they dropped the explanation business.

Gideon could easily have given a very good explanation: an explanation which could have included the fact that God was directing the whole business; and of those who responded to Gideon's first call, only three hundred were accepted anyway. But Gideon did not have to speak any more after he had praised them for their work in capturing Oreb and Zeeb. That was not required to abate their rancor. Their anger was not that noble. All you had to do to cool them off was praise them. Joseph Parker said this showed "that it was a bully's anger, and not a hero's."

Praise has its place, and the Ephraimites were to be commended concerning their victory over the Midianites in the blockade and their capture of Oreb and Zeeb. But if you will only act decent when you are praised, you will not act decent much of the time; for men will not always be so kind and generous as Gideon to give you your due honors. You will get more brickbats than bouquets in life. Therefore, if you are going to behave with grace, you will have to learn how to do it without flowers. Gideon certainly knew how to act without flowers. The Ephraimites had nothing but brickbats for him, but you will notice he behaved well anyway. What a contrast between his behavior and that of the rancorous Ephraimites. May we emulate the performance of Gideon, not that of his tormentors.

3. The Placating was Impermanent

To no discrediting of Gideon, the placating of the Ephraimites' rancor was not permanent. Obviously, if one's rancor is abated not by reasoning but by recognition, it will not last. The

GIDEON

evidence that this placating of the Ephraimites rancor was not permanent occurred some years later when Ephraim pulled the same act with Jephthah, which we briefly referred to earlier. Jephthah judged Israel some fifty years after Gideon judged Israel. After he had led Israel to a great victory over the Ammonites, the Ephraimites "gathered themselves together, and went northward, and said unto Jephthah, Wherefore passedst thou over [the Jordan] to fight against the children of Ammon, and didst not call us to go with thee? we will burn thine house upon thee with fire" (Judges 12:1). Jephthah's glorious victory over the Ammonites upset the Ephraimites just as Gideon's great success over Midian had done years earlier. And it is not difficult to discern that the Ephraimites were upset because they got cut out of the glory which Jephthah had for his victory over the Ammonites. So, like they did with Gideon, they complained that they were not called to battle. Their selfish pride raged again. And it was even worse than in Gideon's time, for this time they said they were going to burn down Jephthah's house.

Ephraim had not learned their lesson under Gideon. Their selfish pride was still very much alive. But it cost them this time. When you do not deal with your sins but let them continue to abide in your heart, the day will come when they will destroy you. The Ephraimites discovered this quite quickly in the way Jephthah responded. He did not respond as Gideon did. "And Jephthah said unto them, I and my people were at great strife with the children of Ammon; and when I called you, ye delivered me not out of their hands. And when I saw that ye delivered me not, I put my life in my hands, and passed over against the children of Ammon, and the LORD delivered them into my hand . . . Then Jephthah gathered together all the men of Gilead, and fought with Ephraim: and the men of Gilead smote Ephraim . . . and there fell at that time of the Ephraimites forty and two thousand" (Judges 12:2,3,4,6).

The Ephraimites got what was coming to them. Both in his answer to the Ephraimites and in his action against them, Jephthah dealt with Ephraim much differently than did Gideon.

Rancor

Gideon had been complimentary to the Ephraimites in his answer, and he took no action. Jephthah was just the opposite. His answer condemned them, and he took severe action against them. We note his answer and action in more detail.

First, in his *answer*, Jephthah condemned the Ephraimites by exposing their fallaciousness. They claimed he had not called them to battle, but that was not true; and Jephthah let them know that in no uncertain terms. He reminded them that they had indeed been called by him to battle—but they would not respond. As we noted earlier, the Ephraimites were the kind that only went to war when the outcome seemed to be obviously in their favor and there was glory to gain. Going to war when Gideon called them to set up a blockade was not difficult because the Midianites were fleeing and at a great disadvantage. But when Jephthah called them to go to war against the Ammonites, the outcome was not yet certain; and so the Ephraimites were not interested. Truly the Psalmist speaks correctly of them when he describes their character, "The children of Ephraim, being armed, and carrying bows, turned back in the day of battle" (Psalm 78:9). No, they did not turn back when victory was assured, but they were not interested in pursuing the battle when victory was uncertain. So Jephthah reminded them of the facts; facts which really condemned the Ephraimites.

Second, in his *action*, Jephthah dealt severely with the Ephraimites and slew thousands of them. Since the Ephraimites were going to burn down his house, Jephthah was forced to take action against them. Before it was over forty-two thousand Ephraimites had died in the confrontation, which is best known for the "Shibboleth" test (Judges 12:5,6). It was a devastating experience for this tribe of Israel, but the Ephraimites had no one to blame but themselves. They were victims of their own selfish pride as much as they were victims of Jephthah's army. "Pride goeth before destruction" (Proverbs 16:18) has few examples that are plainer than that of the Ephraimites.

Those, like the Ephraimites, who see the Lord's work only as a means of self-aggrandizement will be troublers in the camp.

But they will one day experience the heavy hand of Divine judgment. So let every like-minded, disgruntled church member take warning here. Doing so will both help the work of the Lord and secure for them a much better future.

IX.
Retribution

Judges 8:4–21, 28

Gideon's pursuit of complete victory over the Midianites continues and concludes in great success in our present text. Retribution is brought upon the last remnant of the Midianite army, which was completely routed, and upon the two kings of Midian, Zebah and Zalmunna, who are captured and slain. Capturing and slaying the two kings climaxed the great victory over the Midianites, for they were the leaders of the Midianite oppression of Israel.

Our text also tells of severe retribution being brought upon some Israelites for opposing Gideon's final pursuit of the two Midianite kings and the last remnant of the Midianite army. These Israelites discovered that God does not look kindly upon those, even of His own, who would hinder accomplishments in God's work. Sooner or later those who oppose God's work will experience justified retribution for their offending ways.

In the study of this text, which emphasizes retribution, we will consider the provoking of retribution, the pursuit for retribution, and the punishment from retribution.

A. THE PROVOKING OF RETRIBUTION

We already know what provoked retribution upon the Midianites. Here we note what provoked retribution against some Israelites. When Gideon and his three hundred passed over the Jordan River to continue their pursuit of the two Midianite kings and the last survivors of the Midianite army, they were "faint, yet pursuing" (v. 4). Thus, they were in great need of physical nourishment. So Gideon did the customary thing an army would do in those days: he made an appeal for bread to the towns he was passing through. To the leaders of Succoth and Penuel (towns made famous by Jacob traveling through them when he returned to Canaan after twenty years with Laban), Gideon said, "Give, I pray you, loaves of bread unto the people that follow me; for they are faint, and I am pursuing after Zebah and Zalmunna, kings of Midian" (v. 5). But the leaders of these two Israelite towns scornfully refused the request. "And the princes of Succoth said, Are the hands of Zebah and Zalmunna now in thine hand, that we should give bread unto thine army? . . . and the men of Penuel answered him as the men of Succoth had answered him" (vv. 6, 8).

This refusal to help Gideon and his men in their pursuit of the Midianites was a dastardly deed, for it resisted a noble cause and reviled noble conduct. That will provoke justified and severe retribution every time.

1. The Cause Resisted

The seriousness of the the evil in refusing to help Gideon is emphasized by the character of the cause which Gideon represented. He represented a very worthy work. It was the removal of the Midianite oppression of Israel. For seven years, Midian, under the leadership of their two kings, Zebah and Zalmunna, had terribly oppressed Israel. These kings stated their cruel goal very plainly, as the Psalmist reported years later: "Zebah . . . and . . . Zalmunna . . . said, Let us take to ourselves the houses [better translated 'pastures'] of God in possession" (Psalm 83:11,12). For seven years the Midianites succeeded in obtaining their goal, for during that time the Israelites had their pastures possessed by the Midianites, lost most of their harvest to these marauding hordes, and were forced to hide in caves and dens for the safety of their lives. But now the Midianites are being driven out of the land; and Gideon is endeavoring to put a thorough end to this yearly invasion by destroying the last remnants of the Midianite army and by catching and slaying the two kings, the ringleaders of the whole oppression.

This, then, was a very noble cause. It was not a questionable endeavor, an unjustified effort, or an unimportant work. It was a work that would greatly benefit all Israel. In fact, this work was one of the greatest needs that Israel had; and, therefore, it was certainly very worthy of support. For an Israelite to refuse to support this work was more than enough to provoke even the most slowly inspired retribution, for it reflected much degraded character. We note particularly that in rejecting this cause the leaders of Succoth and Penuel acted cowardly, traitorously, and selfishly.

They acted cowardly. It takes boldness to do the work of the Lord; hence, a coward will not stand well against God's enemies. The leaders of Succoth and Penuel lacked boldness to do God's work, and they revealed it by their cowardly answer to Gideon. They said they were not going to help Gideon unless the two kings of Midian were in Gideon's hands. They obviously feared the two kings and were not going to take a stand against them for fear of reprisal if Gideon did not catch them. Succoth and Penuel were not far from the Midianite dwellings and could be easily avenged by the Midianites. The leaders of Succoth and Penuel did not have the courage to deal with that situation nobly.

We have many cowards in Christendom today. They evidence their cowardliness by their refusal to take a stand against evil for fear of some reprisal, such as, a loss of respect, friends, or job. As preachers, they will not speak out against some sins, for they are afraid of losing members or their job. As church members, they will not take action against the evil conduct of some other church member, for they are afraid of losing that member as a friend. These cowards do not have enough spiritual boldness to take much of a stand against any evil; and, therefore, they will be of little help in doing any work that attacks evil. Those who must check to see which way the wind is blowing before they take a stand, only betray their cowardliness.

GIDEON

This cowardliness evidences a lack of faith and it comes from a lack of faith. Faith makes us bold in the Lord's work. As an example, Moses' parents were said to be bold because of faith. "By faith Moses, when he was born, was hid three months of his parents . . . they were not afraid of the king's commandment" (Hebrews 11:23). Moses also was bold because of his faith. "By faith he forsook Egypt, not fearing the wrath of the king" (Hebrews 11:27). So at the root of cowardliness in the Lord's work is unbelief. We may want to disguise our cowardliness to take a stand against evil as a lot of other things, such as charity or prudence; but it still is nothing but wicked unbelief.

They acted traitorously. The people of Succoth and Penuel were Israelites. Yet, they were aiding the enemy by refusing to support the pursuit of Gideon to destroy the enemy. That, plain and simple, is treason! You do not need to unsheathe a sword and stab Gideon in the back to be guilty of treason. You only have to withhold support, and thus make it unnecessarily difficult for Gideon to do his work, in order to be guilty of treason. We need to emphasize this fact today in our country as well as in the churches.

In our country we have some who want to pass themselves off as patriotic, who yet give help and encouragement to the enemy by what they say and do. No, they do not pick up a gun and fire at our soldier boys; but they go on strike in war production plants in time of war, report sensitive information indiscreetly, stir up a hostile spirit against the government by demonstrations, and willingly broadcast enemy propaganda. Draft dodgers, anti-war protesters, flag burners, many news reporters, and other like people are nothing but traitors. Yet in our day of sick ideology, such people are often praised instead of arrested.

This same treasonous attitude is often seen in church, too. Many church members give little support to the church's ministry or withhold it altogether. But if you withhold support from God's work, you are against God; you are a traitor in the church.

RETRIBUTION

Jesus said, "He that is not with me is against me" (Matthew 12:30). If you do not support Him, you are against Him. There is no such thing as being neutral in this business. You are either for or against.

In time of war, treason used to be punishable by death. If God so judged all traitors in the church, a great many of our members would have been dead and gone long ago.

They acted selfishly. Gideon's request was most reasonable. It was not demanding. He only asked for bread. He did not ask the people of Succoth and Penuel to risk their lives and go to battle—although he would have been justified in so asking. Gideon's request was not a burdensome request. And, as Matthew Henry states, "The request would have been reasonable if they had been but poor travelers in distress." Yet, it was spurned. These leaders of Succoth and Penuel were so selfish they would not even part with some bread to help Gideon do a work that would greatly benefit them and all Israel. "These men were blind to the glory of the common cause—selfish, poor-spirited creatures, that shut themselves up in their fenced cities, and were satisfied to let God's soldiers starve, and God's work come to an end for want of support, so long only as they had bread enough to satisfy their own hunger" (Marcus Dods). What wretched selfishness!

Selfishness, among other problems it has, is so shortsighted. It does not realize that it cuts its own throat. Had God not helped Gideon and his three hundred with extra strength, they would not have destroyed the Midianites, which would in turn have caused Succoth and Penuel to eventually lose a lot of their bread to surviving marauding Midianites. Giving to Gideon was not losing bread, but assuring themselves of future bread. But stingy people never see that fact well.

Many of this kind are in church. They are tightwads who will not give much of anything; yet, of course, they are the first to complain if the church does not do well. Such misers in God's work have either never heard of "Give, and it shall be given unto you" (Luke 6:38) or do not believe it. So fearing they will lose by giving, they hold selfishly onto their pocketbooks during offering time, not realizing they are only pickpocketing themselves.

2. The Conduct Reviled

When Gideon appealed for aid from Succoth and Penuel, he and his three hundred had already worked a tremendous work. The Midianites had been routed; and so much so that only 15,000 of an army of 135,000 were left, and they, along with the two kings, were fleeing for their lives. This should have really commended him to the leaders of Succoth and Penuel and secured from them much respect and support. But it did not. The leaders of Succoth and Penuel so scorned the outstanding past performance of Gideon and his men that they refused to show any confidence in their capturing of Zebah and Zalmunna. So they answered, "Are the hands of Zebah and Zalmunna now in thine hand, that we should give bread unto thine army?" This was a mean, verbal slap in the face of Gideon and his men. With this answer they "did upbraid [reproach, scorn, revile]" (v. 15) Gideon and his troops. It discredited all their past achievements as nothing. They would so misrepresent the picture that Gideon and his men come off as talkers but not doers, as men who have not yet done anything worthy of support. The only thing the leaders of Succoth and Penuel talked about was what Gideon and his three hundred had not yet done. Such reviling certainly invites retribution.

We should not be surprised at this attitude about Gideon's work by these leaders of Succoth and Penuel. When folk do not support the work of God, they will not have much good to say about the workers of God. If the work is not respected, neither will the workers be respected, no matter how much good they do. Anyone who would serve the Lord in His work will quickly find this out. They will quickly discover the contempt many have, even in church, for their work. Their accomplishments, though great they may be, will often be totally ignored; but what they have not done will be made the issue. So the pastor, who works from morning till night and is "faint, yet pursuing" his duties, will be called on the phone by some mean-spirited church member and criticized for something he did not get done. No credit is given for the many, many things he has accomplished. Rather the emphasis is placed on what he did not do. Furthermore, no consideration is given for the fact that the harassed pastor cannot do everything his people think he ought to do even if he had twice as many hours in each day. Revilers of excellence in the Lord's work are indeed a most inconsiderate bunch.

Gideon learned here what he had learned in his trouble with the Ephraimites and what every dedicated soul eventually learns, namely, that those who claim to be God's people are often as big a hindrance to God's work as are the ungodly. They will discourage you, get in your the way, and endeavor to stop others from helping you in your spiritual pursuit. But such reviling conduct is dangerous business. It only sets one up for Divine retribution, as it did the leaders of Succoth and Penuel.

B. THE PURSUIT FOR RETRIBUTION

The pursuit by Gideon to bring lasting retribution upon the remnant of the Midianite army and upon the two kings of Midian, was both a very steadfast and a very successful pursuit. And the steadfastness of the pursuit was an important key to the successfulness of the pursuit. Before success was steadfastness. That is always the case. True success always includes the prerequisite of steadfastness. This truth is found repeatedly in the Bible. As an example, this truth is seen in the message God gave Joshua about success. "This book of the law shall not depart out of thy mouth [steadfastness of speaking]; but thou shalt mediate therein day and night [steadfastness of meditation], that thou mayest observe to do according to all [steadfastness of conduct] that is written therein: for then [after steadfastness has been duly practiced] . . . thou shalt have good success" (Joshua 1:8).

We will look separately at both the steadfastness of the pursuit and the success of the pursuit in order to learn some helpful lessons for any pursuit in God's work.

1. The Steadfastness of the Pursuit

The steadfastness of Gideon and his three hundred men in the pursuit of complete victory was exceptional. It was a steadfastness that would not be satisfied with partial victory and would not be stopped by difficulties.

Not satisfied with partial victory. As we noted in our previous chapter, Gideon believed in total victory. Therefore, he would not quit his pursuit until he had completely defeated the Midianites. He would continue his pursuit here until he had "discomforted all the host" (v. 12) of the remaining soldiers of Midian's army and captured and killed the two kings of Midian. If Gideon had been like many today, he would have quit before he had finished the job. Some would have quit as soon as the Midianites started fleeing the valley of Jezreel. Many would certainly have quit at the Jordan after the Ephraimites handed Gideon the heads of Oreb and Zeeb. After all, the power of Midian had been greatly reduced by then. Only 15,000 remained of the 135,000 men who drew sword (v. 10), and they were fleeing back to their homeland east of the Jordan. But Gideon wanted to eradicate the Midianite problem. He wanted to take every Midianite cancer cell out of Israel. He wanted no germs in the body. He saw beyond today and considered tomorrow also. "He would not have the plain of Jezreel again the prey of those locusts from the east. And so Midian must be crushed" (A. C. Hervey).

Lack of commitment to total victory plagues Christianity today. We are too easily satisfied in the spiritual realm. In the secular and material world—especially in sports—we seem much more interested in going all out for victory. But, unfortunately, we are so carnal that in the spiritual arena we often quit before we have begun because we do not care about complete victory. Hence, we do half-way jobs, we do just enough to get by for today, we never quite overcome our evil habits, and with this lack of commitment we keep our churches from really doing business in a great way for God. We are like King Joash, who, before Elisha, smote the ground with the arrows only three times rather than five or six times and thus did not gain complete victory over Syria.

If anyone does indicate their interest in total victory by an exceptional faithfulness and dedication to the Word, prayer, worship, and service, that person is quickly criticized and put in the category of a fanatic; and others are warned not to be like that person but to have a "balanced" life. Gideon's attitude about total victory is simply not popular. But it is useless to lament our futility when we oppose his commitment.

Not stopped by difficulties. Gideon "effected his purpose [of successfully pursuing the Midianites] under the greatest disadvantages" (Matthew Henry). Great difficulties did not stop him. "Yet pursuing" (v. 4) characterized Gideon's steadfast efforts in spite of difficulties—difficulties which can be summed up in a fourfold way. He was not only "faint [exhausted, weak], yet pursuing" (Ibid.), where most writers seem to put the emphasis; but he was also few in number "yet pursuing," unsupported by his people "yet pursuing," and criticized in his work "yet pursuing" where we need to put equal emphasis.

These four difficulties Gideon faced, though great, are not uncommon ones. So we will look in more detail at these four problems in order to encourage our own steadfastness.

First, he was *weak in strength*. "Gideon . . . and the three hundred men that were with him, [were] faint, yet pursuing" (v. 4). How that statement rebukes our lack of dedication in the Lord's work. This was a difficulty which came about because of great dedication—a difficulty the slothful in service know nothing about. He was not faint through delinquency, but faint through duty.

In dedicated pursuit of his duty, Gideon and his army experienced faintness through lack of sleep—they were up all night;

through lack of taking in any nourishment—they had no time to eat; and through the expending of great amounts of energy—they had traveled at a very energetic pace some twenty-five or more miles by foot all the way from the valley of Jezreel down the Jordan Valley and across the Jordan fighting the Midianites. No wonder they were exhausted. They were not weary of the work, but they certainly were weary in the work.

Faintness, regardless of how meritoriously it occurs, does, however, become a problem. It slows our pace, weakens our efforts, and can dampen our spirit. Gideon sought relief from Succoth and Penuel but did not get it. However, the Lord supplied the need. As we will note later, God infused Gideon and his men with additional strength; or they never would have been able to successfully continue their pursuit. "Out of weakness were made strong" (Hebrews 11:34) certainly illustrates the experience of Gideon and his three hundred. And God will do the same for us. When we have expended our energies in His work, He will not leave us alongside the road no longer wanted. God promises us in His Word that "they that wait upon the LORD shall renew their strength" (Isaiah 40:31) and "I can do all things through Christ, which strengtheneth me" (Philippians 4:13) and "my strength is made perfect in weakness" (II Corinthians 12:9).

Second, he was *few in number*. Though a great many Midianites had already been slain, Gideon was still outnumbered 50 to 1 when his 300 went after the remaining 15,000 of Midian. But numbers are not imperative to do God's work, for God said, "If ye walk in my statutes, and keep my commandments, and do them . . . five of you shall chase an hundred, and an hundred of you shall put ten thousand to flight: and your enemies shall fall before you" (Leviticus 26:3,8). Neither do numbers validate a cause. In fact, in this world, numbers generally invalidate a cause; for what is popular in this world is generally not godly. That which is godly frequently has little following, for God's cause has seldom had impressive numbers on its side. So, though discouraging it may appear, the lack of numbers need not stop us from doing God's work. As long as we are on God's side, we have enough numbers to conquer and to be victorious.

Third, he was *unsupported by his people*. Gideon's small army was exhausted from their long rigorous fighting and were in need of food. But they were turned down by the people of Succoth and Penuel when he asked for food. It is very difficult to keep going when God's people refuse to support us. How shameful that Gideon's own people would not support him. But this problem is not unique to Gideon's day. Missionaries and pastors and other Christian workers are acquainted with this problem, too. Meager salaries and partial support constantly plague the ministry. But God's servants must not quit the fight when others will not help them. They must look up to the One Who will never fail to help them.

Fourth, he was *criticized in his work*. We have earlier noted in detail some of this problem, but we want to mention it again here; for it was one of the difficulties Gideon had to overcome if he was to be steadfast in his work.

Gideon got repeated doses of this treatment. Gideon first experienced this treatment from the Ephraimites, while he was pursuing the Midianites. They had very critical, but unjustified, things to say to him. This does not encourage continuance in the work. But Gideon did not stop. Then he got some more of the same treatment from Succoth and Penuel. In refusing to support him, they criticized his work by saying he had not done enough to merit their support. But Gideon would not let that stop him either. Neither must we. If we would serve steadfastly and hence faithfully, we will have to ignore the criticism of our work by others.

2. The Success of the Pursuit

"And Gideon . . . smote the host: for the host was secure . . . and took the two kings of Midian, Zebah and Zalmunna, and discomforted all the host . . . Thus was Midian subdued before the children of Israel, so that they lifted up their heads no more" (vv. 11, 12, 28). Great success accompanied Gideon's pursuit. He accomplished his objectives to the fullest.

We want to note the miracle in the success, the warning in the success, and the encouragement in the success.

The miracle in the success. Gideon and his three hundred could not have accomplished this great success of destroying the last 15,000 warriors of the Midianites and capturing the two kings if they had not experienced a miracle of Divine strengthening. Many overlook the miracle of Divine strengthening in this pursuit. But it had to be there or Gideon and his men would not have succeeded in this pursuit. Gideon and his three hundred needed the miracle. They were already "faint" before they made the final pursuit of the remaining hosts of Midianites and the two kings, and their appeal for bread was denied, so they had to continue their pursuit on empty stomachs. Thus, under these conditions, the only way they could accomplish what they did was for God to give them some miracle strength.

Therefore, the fight against the Midianites began with a miracle (when the three hundred routed the multiplied thousands with nothing more than a trumpet, broken pitcher, torch, and a battle cry); and it ended with a miracle (when God gave them extra strength). Truly, Gideon, as we noted in the previous chapter, could no longer lament "where are all his [God's] miracles" (Judges 6:13).

The warning in the success. "The host was secure" (v. 11) when Gideon came upon them. This means the Midianites thought they had escaped from Gideon and no longer needed to worry about his attacking them. Smug and complacent, they were not expecting him, nor were they ready for him. So it was a great shock for them when suddenly Gideon came upon them. They had no chance to escape, and Gideon quickly "smote" them (v. 12).

The unsuspecting Midianite, thinking himself secure when he was not, pictures many a sinner. Wilson says that the word "secure" means "to trust, to confide in, to rely upon; to be confident, i.e. secure, without fear." He adds that when the word is used in a negative sense, as it is here, it means to "place trust and confidence in the things of this world, and have no fear of God or of his punishments." This is exactly what many sinners often do. They think they can flee away from the responsibility of their sin and escape judgment. They do not concern themselves about the judgment of God. But sooner or later it will come. None will escape. Unless a man comes to God and seeks peace with Him through Jesus Christ, he will one day suddenly meet up with judgment just as the Midianites did. Sin will be punished. No sinner will escape. He may feel secure in church membership, in acceptance by his peers, and in a deadened conscience. But that security will prove to be extremely false. The only security against Divine judgment is Jesus Christ.

The encouragement in the success. Gideon's success is a great encouragement to every saint that it is possible to live victoriously for the Lord even in the most difficult of times. We need that encouragement today because our world does not give much promise to godliness. Evil seems to have firm and permanent control of things today, as the Midianites did for seven years in Israel. In our own country we watch the promoters of all kinds of evil thrive. Laws are passed to protect and support their evil ways. Homosexuality, alcohol, gambling, abortion, and the ruling of God out of our schools have taken over and with power; while it appears righteousness is not only losing the battle but has little hope of ever conquering evil. However, we must not be discouraged and give up. There is a name before which all evil will bow and be vanquished. It is the name of Jesus Christ, the Captain of our Salvation. He is the Great Gideon of all times; and just when evil thinks it is secure, just when evil thinks it has this world in its absolute control and can stamp out every trace of righteousness, then Christ will suddenly come back to the earth and evil will be destroyed with dispatch. Righteousness will then rule as never before.

But we do not have to wait until that great day when Christ

GIDEON

comes back to experience a Gideon-type victory. We can still do the great things through the power of God today. Though many are the evil Midianite foes, and many are our difficulties; yet, with steadfast faith in God, we can still accomplish the impossible. If Gideon can rout the Midianites with the few he had and in spite of the difficulties he faced, then we too can accomplish great things for God though we may seem to have great disadvantages. That is the great encouraging message of Gideon's success.

C. THE PUNISHMENT FROM RETRIBUTION

We have just noted the final retribution upon the last remnant of the Midianite army, now we will look at the retribution that came upon the leaders of two towns of Israel for their failure to support Gideon and his men, and also the retribution that came upon the two kings of Midian for their murder of Gideon's brothers. The retribution which came upon these people is given in detail, unlike that of the last segment of the Midianite army.

The retribution punishment upon the leaders of Succoth and Penuel comes first in order in the Scripture; then the retribution upon the two kings of Midian is recorded.

1. The Punishment of the Israelite Leaders

When Gideon finished destroying the Midianite forces and had captured the two kings of Midian, he returned to Succoth and Penuel to carry out the punishment he had promised earlier when they had refused to support his pursuit. He "caught a young man of the men of Succoth, and inquired of him: and he described unto him the names of the princes of Succoth, and the elders thereof, even threescore and seventeen men. And he came unto the men of Succoth, and said, Behold Zebah and Zalmunna, with whom ye did upbraid me, saying, Are the hands of Zebah and Zalmunna now in thine hand, that we should give bread unto thy men that are weary? And he took the elders of the city, and thorns of the wilderness and briers, and with them he taught the men of Succoth. And he beat down the tower of

Retribution

Penuel, and slew the men of the city" (vv. 14–17). The punishment Gideon gave these leaders was severe, just, and gracious.

Severe. The leaders of Succoth and Penuel were all slain. Succoth's leaders were slain through a bloody tearing of the flesh by "thorns of the wilderness and briers," which was according to F. C. Cook, "A mode of capital punishment." Penuel's leaders were slain when the tower they were hiding in for protection was beaten down by Gideon and his men.

Some do not think Succoth's leaders were slain because of the "with them [thorns and briers] he taught the men of Succoth" (v. 16). However, since Gideon slew all the leaders of Penuel, "this makes it probable that the . . . [punishment] of the men of Succoth was a capital punishment, as there is no reason why the men of Penuel should be more severely punished than the men of Succoth" (A. C. Hervey). Furthermore, "taught," which means "to know; to cause to know" (Wilson), does not necessarily prohibit capital punishment here, for these men would not have to be spared to learn they were being judged for their sin. Countless multitudes have been taught by God over the years through their own judgmental deaths. That, however, is the worst time to finally learn, for it is too late to use the learning to your own advantage. Of course the living can still learn from the judgment of those who die. "It was too late for their [the guilty] good, but not for the instruction and warning of others" (Matthew Poole).

The severity of the punishment emphasizes the seriousness of their sin. These leaders would not support God's cause, and they reviled God's servants. In our day folk do not seem to realize the seriousness of this sort of conduct. The way people act in church in withholding their support for the work and in their mistreatment of the pastor and other Christian workers, you would think this sort of opposition was not a transgression, or if it is a sin then it is just a slight transgression at the most. But it is not! It is a great sin. And many are those whom God has dealt with severely for their dissident ways. Unfortunately, when judgment does come, it is explained away as being a result of something else and is seldom associated with rebellion against God's work and workers. But if the truth were known, more sicknesses, accidents, hardships, and troubles have come upon church members because of this problem than what church people want to admit. It ought to make one shudder when he opposes God's work and worker, but few people fear that sin today.

Just. There are many who are critical of the judgment Gideon brought upon the leaders of Succoth and Penuel. Even some very respected writers indict Gideon here and accuse him of being proud, vindictive, and unholy in the way he punished these leaders. The criticism against Gideon is both for the severity of the retribution (death) and for the form he used to bring the retribution (briers and thorns for Succoth, and beating down a tower to kill the men of Penuel). But much of that criticism follows the attitude of today which goes easy on crime. Furthermore, most of the critics forget the seriousness of the crime of which these leaders of Succoth and Penuel were guilty—which was treason. But regardless of the critics, Gideon was just in his actions. Both the form of the punishment and the severity of the punishment can be easily justified.

First, the *form of the punishment* was, of course, not the form we would use today. We would use such things as the electric chair, gas chamber, hanging, or the firing squad. But Gideon used what was available and what was practiced in his day.

For Succoth he used the thorn and brier method, an unusual method to us but not to them. There is uncertainty just as to how this form of punishment was executed and what all was involved. But it evidently did not take long and would certainly be a sobering warning to the innocent observer.

For Penuel he simply destroyed the tower in which the men of Penuel had sought protection from retribution. It was the only way he could punish Penuel; for these men, by their hiding, forced this method upon Gideon.

Gideon cannot be faulted in the form of punishment he

used. It fit the day and the occasion. He did not resort to some unusual form just to be mean and nasty.

Second, the *severity of the punishment* fit the crime. These leaders were guilty of treason. Treason has always been a crime that is punishable by death, especially in a time of war; and it should be, for it is a crime that can cause many innocents to perish. Had Gideon not been able to defeat "all the host" (v. 12), many Israelites would have died in future marauding raids of the surviving Midianites. Charles Simeon says, in justification of the severe punishment, "Now we say that this [punishment] was just. Had the injury which he [Gideon] had sustained been purely personal, it would have become him to pass it by . . . But he acted as a magistrate who was authorized to punish the treason of which these persons had been guilty . . . It was treason, both against the state, and against God . . . It [the refusal to support Gideon] was the very way to prevent the execution of Gideon's designs against the enemies of God and his people."

When prone to criticize the severity of the punishment of criminals, we need to start considering more the seriousness of their crime. Especially is this true in regards to capital punishment. No method of capital punishment seems anything but brutal, for taking of life is not pretty. But capital punishment is ordained of God and necessary. Some will always find fault with capital punishment because life-taking is severe. But the critics forget that the crime is worse, for crime affects *innocent* people; capital punishment, in contrast, affects *evil* people. The disgusting protest over the severity of the punishment given criminals today does not show much charity for the victim. We are protecting the criminal more than the victim, but such action will destroy any institution in the land. The home, the church, the school, and the government are all paying a great price because we are unwilling to deal out just judgment upon the criminal. Gideon's retribution may be unpalatable to many, but it fit the crime and did the job—something our lenient ways are not doing at all.

Gideon

Gracious. Now some will wonder how we can say the punishment was gracious when it was the death sentence. Easy; the punishment was delayed after it was announced. When the leaders of Succoth and Penuel refused to help Gideon, he warned them, "Therefore when the LORD hath delivered Zebah and Zalmunna into mine hand, then [and not until then] I will tear your flesh with the thorns of the wilderness and with briers . . . .And he spoke also unto the men of Penuel, saying, When [and not until when] I come again in peace [after he had established peace by defeating the Midianite army and capturing Zebah and Zalmunna], I will break down this tower [in which the men of Penuel thought they could protect themselves]" (vv. 7,9). Gideon did not punish these leaders at the moment they refused to help him. His first priority, at that time, was to finish off the Midianites. Then when that was accomplished, he would come back and take care of the punishment.

This delay was an act of grace. It gave the leaders time to repent. This is God's way. People often are very critical of God when He judges men, but they seldom consider the fact that God gives men ample time to repent. "God gives notice of danger, and space to repent, that sinners may flee from the wrath to come" (Matthew Henry). A classic example of grace in judgment is found in Revelation 2:21 concerning Jezebel. Even vile Jezebel was given grace. "And I gave her space to repent of her fornication, and she repented not." Judgment only comes when grace is rejected. Let men not forget that fact. Hell will be populated by people who spurned God's gracious warning about judgment upon sin. He gave them time to repent but they would not. The problem is not a cruel God; the problem is a grace-rejecting, unrepenting man.

We also need to note here that the delay in the punishment exonerated Gideon from the critics' charge of executing these people because he lost his temper. If Gideon had lost his temper over the reviling rejection of Succoth and Penuel, he would never have waited to execute these leaders of Succoth and Penuel. He would have executed them right on the spot. But

Retribution

Gideon was not controlled by unrestrained passion. He was a man who was most exemplary in the way he controlled his emotions, and he really demonstrated it in first pursuing the Midianites and the coming back to give Succoth and Penuel just retribution.

2. The Punishment of the Midianite Leaders

The final act of retribution occurs when the two kings of Midian are slain. (A plurality of kings was not unusual in Midian—Numbers 31:8 reports a time when Midian once had five kings at one time). We note the revelation in the punishment and the rightness of the punishment.

The revelation in the punishment. Retribution, by the hand of Gideon, came upon Zebah and Zalmunna because they had murdered Gideon's brothers. "Then said he unto Zebah and Zalmunna, What manner of men were they whom ye slew at Tabor? And they answered, As thou art, so were they; each one resembled the children of a king [some flattery here in hopes of gaining mercy]. And he said, They were my brethren, even the sons of my mother: as the LORD liveth, if ye had saved them alive, I would not slay you" (vv. 18,19). This slaying of Gideon's brothers, by these two kings, was an incident that had not heretofore been reported in Scripture. It, therefore, sheds light on some of the bloody brutality which accompanied the oppression of the Israelites by the Midianites. Gideon's brothers evidently were hiding out in Mount Tabor when the Israelites were forced to hide in dens, caves, etc. (Judges 6:2). But, as must have been the case with many Israelites, they were discovered and murdered. Gideon's brothers, particularly, were murdered by these two kings of Midian.

What a good lesson here on "be sure your sin will find you out" (Numbers 32:23). Zebah and Zalmunna had committed this crime earlier but had escaped. Doubtless, they thought they were home free when they got across the Jordan and then to the eastern border of Israel in the security of their own dwelling places. But sin cannot be forever hidden. In this case Gideon found them, captured them, and executed them. Sin committed some time before finally caught up with them. It always does. Retribution upon evil is certain; and the only escape from Divine retribution for sin is through Jesus Christ, Who in order to be our Savior had to experience retribution in our place.

The rightness of the punishment. Not as many criticize Gideon in this judgment as they do in his judgment upon the leaders of Succoth and Penuel. But some still find fault. One thing they particularly fault Gideon for is ordering his son, Jether, to slay the two kings. "And he said unto Jether his firstborn, Up, and slay them" (v. 20). However, as Jamieson said, "A magistrate might order anyone to do the work of the executioner." And Gideon was indeed a magistrate. He was Israel's judge—and Divinely appointed at that. He, therefore, had the proper authority to order the execution and to choose who would execute the kings.

Why did he choose Jether? Gideon "commanded his firstborn son Jether to slay them, for the purpose of adding [to the disgrace of their defeat and capture] the disgrace of falling by the hand of a boy" (Keil). In those days honor was affected by whom the executioner was, by whom the person was that killed you. The lower the rank or esteem of the executioner, the more the shame for the executed. So Gideon ordering Jether, his son, to kill the kings was done "that the death of those mischievous persons might be more shameful" (Matthew Poole). The Midianite kings would not only be shamed by defeat but by the one who executed them.

Gideon's son, however, was not ready to perform such a deed. He was too young to be soldier-toughened and ready for the ordeal of execution, so Gideon went ahead and fulfilled his own sentence upon the men. "But the youth drew not his sword: for he feared, because he was yet a youth . . . And Gideon arose, and slew Zebah and Zalmunna" (vv. 20,21).

The criticism of this retribution again points out the wrong emphasis of those who are forever complaining about punishment given criminals. Those who get upset about this execution need instead to get upset about how much evil was done because of these kings. Not only were they murderers themselves, but they were the ringleaders of the whole invasion by the Midianites which brought so much havoc and suffering for the Israelites. If one is going to criticize—criticize the criminals! These kings deserved the retribution which came upon them; so will every sinner.

Retribution is not the most pleasant subject, and preachers often steer far away from judgment preaching. But retribution against evil is righteous; and if we really want to help people, we would stop condemning retribution and start condemning the evil which makes retribution necessary.

X.
REQUESTS

JUDGES 8:22–27

THE WAR WITH the Midianites is over. Israel is now free from the great oppression which they experienced for seven long years. Gideon, who not many weeks earlier was a nobody ("I am the least in my father's house"), is now a great hero, the "mighty man of valor" (6:12) the angel of the Lord said he was. With this change in circumstance, the people make a request of Gideon, who in turn makes a request of them. They want him to have dominion over them, and he wants them to make a donation to him.

These two requests are fraught with perils and problems. It would have been better if each request had not been made. They were not a good aftermath of the war with Midian. They revealed that Israel still had some serious spiritual problems, and they laid the groundwork for great problems for Israel in the future. These requests tell us that we need more than a victory over Midian to solve the problems of our land. We also need victory over the flesh. But few folk ever see that vital need. Give them a victory over Midian; and they think their problems are solved, when, in fact, the root of their problems may not have been adequately addressed at all.

A. THE DOMINION REQUEST

"Then the men of Israel said unto Gideon, Rule thou over us, both thou, and thy son, and thy son's son also: for thou hast delivered us from the hand of Midian" (v. 22). This was quite a request. The men of Israel were requesting Gideon to be their king. But they did not stop there, they also requested that he set up a dynasty—that is, after he dies the throne would be passed on to his son and then to his grandson, etc.

We will consider the recognition in the request, the reason behind the request, and the refusal of the request.

1. The Recognition in the Request

Gideon was asked to be king because "thou hast delivered us from the hand of Midian." There is both a deserving recognition and a deficient recognition in this request.

A deserving recognition. The request recognizes the good work Gideon had done. There is a place for giving "honor to whom honor" (Romans 13:7) is due. The Word instructs us to honor certain people. We are to "Honor thy father and thy mother" (Exodus 20:12); we are to honor our elders (Leviticus 19:32); servants are to honor their masters (I Timothy 6:1); and those who minster well in the Word are to be counted worthy of "double honor" (I Timothy 5:17). So Gideon, who had served the Lord with excellence, needs to be properly honored by the people. It speaks well of the people to give him some recognition. We have noticed in previous studies that some of the Israelites were not doing well in this area. The Ephraimites had shown much uncalled-for rancor against him, and the leaders of Succoth and Penuel had reviled him. But now Gideon is finally receiving some due accolades, some due recognition.

One of the problems in our day is that we often honor the wrong kind of people for the wrong kind of things. We honor actors, pop stars, ballplayers, and celebrities who have little character and whose work and achievements are nothing to honor. In fact, many of the achievements which have made these people famous—and thus recognized with honors—are downright iniquitous. Gideon had some worthy accomplishments which justified his being recognized. He was a person whose achievements were noble, God-honoring, and truly beneficial to his fellow men. However, such people seldom get honors today; or like Gideon, they have to first experience much hostility before they are properly honored.

What the Israelites said to Gideon can be and needs to be said by every saint to Jesus Christ. "Rule thou over us . . . for thou hast delivered us" fits Jesus Christ better than it does anyone else. Christ has redeemed us from our sins; He has saved us from eternal condemnation; He was the One that "wast slain, and hast redeemed us to God by thy blood" (Revelation 5:9). Therefore, He should be our Ruler; He should have chief dominion over us. We owe it to Him. Furthermore, asking Him to rule over us is a request, unlike the people's request of Gideon, that is definitely not fraught with perils and problems for us spiritually. In fact, it is the best situation we can have in our life.

A deficient recognition. In the honoring of Gideon by recognizing his work against Midian, the men of Israel left out God. It was proper for them to honor Gideon; but in the victory over Midian, they needed to honor God first and foremost. He was the main reason Israel overcame Midian. He had worked tremendous miracles to save Israel and to destroy the Midianites. But these men of Israel said not a word about God's great work in the deliverance from the Midianites.

The men of Israel should have said to God what they said to Gideon. But there was no mention about submitting to God because of the great work He had done in delivering Israel. Yet, this was their great need; for their great problem, which resulted in the Midianite oppression, was their unwillingness to let God rule in their hearts and lives and land. But these men were not focusing well on God at all. Rather "These men were so dazzled by the splendor of human achievement that they ignored the Divine influence which was the source of them. Gideon's campaign was especially designed to avoid the danger of people attributing to men what was really the work of God [cp. 7:2 where the army was reduced from 32,000 to 300, 'lest Israel vaunt themselves against me, saying, Mine own hand hath saved me'] . . . Yet they regarded Gideon as the sole hero, and forgot to glorify God" (W. F. Adeney).

Men are prone to honor anyone but God. "We are all too ready to recognize the human instrument only, and ignore the divine power which is the source of all that is good and great" (W. F. Adeney). Sometimes men are deficient in giving due recognition to men, as we noted above; but the most deficient recognition of all is the recognition men give God. And not only are men poor in recognizing God properly, but often they also become insistent on not giving God any recognition at all. We see some of this detestable attitude in those who pervert our nation's Constitution to the extent that it is used to stop the mentioning and honoring of God in our schools and places of government. Men (particularly the ACLU) go to court and fervently insist that we should not in any way recognize or honor God in these places. How terrible. Yea, how eternally tragic for those who so strongly oppose the honoring of God.

2. The Reason Behind the Request

Why did Israel want a king? We know why they chose Gideon for the position, for he had "delivered us from the hand of Midian." But why did they want a king in the first place? The answer will be found in I Samuel where Israel is recorded as continually requesting that Samuel, the last judge, provide them a king. Their repeated request plainly stated the reason they wanted a king. They said, "We will have a king over us; That we also may be like all the nations; that our king may judge us, and go out before us, and fight our battles" (I Samuel 8:19,20). Israel wanted to be like other nations—that was the main reason for their desire to have a king. "There was a constant tendency in Israel to have [want] a visible ruler, some one like all the nations, who would lead them forth to battle, and reign over them in times of peace" (Ridout). But it was an unholy desire. It rejected God; "they have rejected me, that I should not reign over them" (I Samuel 8:7) was God's comment about the repeated request.

GIDEON

In the time of the Judges, Israel did not have a king. They were under a theocracy which is a government in which God is the main ruler. Judges existed at that time, but they were not accorded the great power of a king. Their chief work was delivering Israel from their enemies. While they were accorded some legal authority which, as an example, permitted them to execute criminals, as we noted with Gideon, they were more advisory in their position than dictatorial which is a contrast to a king. A king is extremely dictatorial. A king rules by fiat; a judge simply exhorts or pleads with the people. But though the rule of a judge gave more liberty to a people than the rule of a king, the Israelites did not want the rule of the judges. They wanted a king. There was more glory, pomp, and prestige in a king than a judge, and that greatly appealed to the flesh. The king was a rallying point for the people. But God wanted to be the main Ruler of Israel. He wanted Israel to rally around Him, glory in Him, and look to Him for victory. But this was too spiritual for the people. It was not what other nations did, and so they persisted in their request for a king until they got one when Samuel was judge in the land.

But, oh, what a disaster they got in Saul, their first king. What a warning it is on wanting to be like the world and also on insisting in having one's own way and not God's way. We all need this warning, for we all often want to be like the world. We too often admire their God-forbidden ways and means, methods and procedures, vestments and decor, and glitter and grandeur. And we all want our own way frequently, too. Self-will is favored over God's will but to our great loss.

3. The Refusal of the Request

The most noble thing about this dominion request was the refusal of it by Gideon. In fact, Gideon's refusal is viewed by others as his best moment. A. F. Muir said that in this refusal "His humility and magnanimous loyalty to God as [the] only Sovereign for Israel outshine all his exploits." William Burrows said this refusal was "Gideon at his best." And W. Miller said,

Requests

"His rejection of it [the throne] was the climax of his moral and spiritual glory."

Gideon's refusal of this request is a great lesson how to obtain victory over temptation. The request was a great temptation; for it urged upon Gideon a very attractive situation which was, as we already noted, plainly wrong. So the refusal demonstrated how to overcome temptation. We will look here at both the character of the temptation and the conquering of the temptation in order to gain some valuable instruction on the subject of temptation.

The character of the temptation. We note four things about this temptation which we see in many temptations and which makes any temptation very strong, appealing, and difficult to refuse.

First, the temptation was *popular*. Gideon was approached by the "men of Israel." Representatives of Israel's tribes, if not all the tribes then at least those tribes especially affected by the Midianite oppression, came to Gideon to make the request. Therefore, it was a request of the populace. It was the voice of the people. It was a very popular movement in the land.

How very strong is temptation when it advocates what is popular with man. Few can resist a temptation when all the people seem to be voicing strong support for it. But we must remember that the saying, *vox populi, vox Dei* (the voice of the people, is the voice of God), is not true. Rather, the voice of the people is an untrustworthy voice. Therefore, "We must not mold our character simply in obedience to the dictates of public opinion. The wish of the people is no excuse for doing wrong (W. F. Adeney). But popularity makes temptation exceedingly strong, for most people are more concerned with what's popular with man than what's right. Whether God approves or applauds means nothing to the average man on the street.

Second, the temptation was *rewarding*. This temptation offered Gideon much. It offered him personal fame, honor, power, and wealth; and it promised the same for his family.

These things are extremely hard to turn down. They encompass just about everything the flesh seeks after in life. Temptation always tries to convince us that there is great compensation for yielding. Money, promotion, security, power, status, pleasure, luxuries, and a host of other things are compensations which temptation holds out to the tempted as inducements to yield to the temptation. However, the catch is that temptation also has other compensations for yielding—compensations better described as evil consequences. Temptation, of course, tries to conceal these compensations. But those who yield to temptation will soon discover these untold evil consequences, and they will discover that these consequences will far exceed the promised rewarding compensations. In fact, the promised rewards will often be found to be a mirage, a lie, empty talk, and a mean trick just to destroy you. Beware of the promises of temptation; they are ever so deceitful.

Third, the temptation was *plausible*. The request implied that Israel had a great need which Gideon could meet. Those making the offer felt that Israel definitely needed a king. It sounded good on the surface. After all, temptation would argue, a nation needs to have authority, government, and rule. It would not be good to be without a ruler; for the nation would then be weak, vulnerable to the enemy, disorganized, and inefficient. Yes, temptation would insist, we must have a better government and surely Gideon is the man; for he delivered the nation from terrible oppression. Let Gideon and his sons and sons' sons rule, and we will be victors over our enemies forever.

However, they did not need a better government. They already had a theocracy, and God is the best Ruler of all. But temptation, in order to strengthen its appeal and power, often makes itself look necessary and urgent. It wants you to think it is imperative that you yield. Therefore, it is not surprising that we often hear people justifying their wayward ways by insisting they have no other choice than to do what they are doing, which is, however, wrong.

Temptation ever tries to make circumstances justify evil

conduct. Circumstances may indeed guide some of our conduct, but circumstances are not that which decide right and wrong. Our code of conduct must be higher than circumstances; it must be the commands of God if we are going to thwart temptation.

Fourth, the temptation was *timely*. One of the most vulnerable times for temptation to strike is at the time of some success. "There are few who will pause in a moment of high personal success to think of the point of morality involved" (R. A. Watson). When we reach the mountain peak of success, the air is thin; and if we are not careful and cautious, we will get heady, dizzy, and then fall.

There are two things which often accompany success which can especially make us vulnerable to temptation. They are euphoria and pride. Euphoria has a tendency to lessen our caution. In our success we become excited, jubilant; and we celebrate. Our spirits soar, but this does not promote caution. Thus temptation has an advantage. Lack of caution always gives temptation an advantage. Pride also makes us an easy pushover for temptation. "Pride goeth before destruction, and an haughty spirit before a fall" (Proverbs 16:18). King Uzziah was made an easy target of temptation because of the pride which accompanied his success. "He was marvelously helped, till he was strong. But when he was strong, his heart was lifted up to his destruction" (II Chronicles 26:15,16). Success is not necessarily evil, but it can be a very vulnerable time for temptation to strike successfully if due caution is not practiced.

The conquering of the temptation. Gideon's refusal of the request to be the king of Israel is a great example of how to refuse temptation, how to conquer evil instead of being conquered by it. We note three important ways in which Gideon defeated temptation which are ways we, too, can defeat temptation. Gideon was adamant, self-denying, and God-honoring.

First, he was *adamant*. Gideon's answer was very firm, forceful, and plain. He said, "I will not rule over you, neither shall my son rule over you." There was no tongue in the cheek

GIDEON

"maybe" here. It was "no" all the way. Gideon was not like some politicians when asked if they are going to run for the presidency or some other office. They do not give a clear cut acceptance, but they do not really refuse either. Such an answer means they can be talked into running for the presidency. But Gideon was not like that; no one had to guess at what he meant. They never asked Gideon again if he would be king, for he slammed the door shut with his adamant refusal.

The only way to answer temptation successfully is with a firm, forceful "No." Anything less than that and you have let temptation stick its foot in the door, and you will then have great difficulty in trying to close the door to temptation. Some will complain that Gideon's answer was discourteously abrupt and blunt, and that he should have used softer language lest he offend the people. But you owe no respect to that which tempts you to evil. Remember if temptation wins, it will treat you with utter disdain.

Charles Spurgeon did not worry about niceties when he rejected a tempting offer from P. T. Barnum. Barnum had invited Spurgeon to come to America to speak in a large tent in Barnum's traveling circus. He made a very attractive offer to Spurgeon which included paying Spurgeon one thousand dollars per lecture—very big money in those days! Barnum, of course, would get the rest of the gate receipts, which Barnum felt would be very large, for Spurgeon was well known and crowds thronged his church. In Spurgeon's letter of response to Barnum, he wrote, "You will find my answer in Acts 13:10." Acts 13:10 says, "O full of all subtility and all mischief, thou child of the devil, thou enemy of all righteousness, wilt thou not cease to pervert the right ways of the Lord?" That is strong language. Some would really have scolded Spurgeon for such strong and offensive language. But you will note that Spurgeon did not sully his character. Many, however, who seem so afraid they may offend some in opposing temptation are a different story.

Second, he was *self-denying*. To refuse this temptation, Gideon had to deny himself many attractive things which people today are just not in the habit of denying themselves. Lack of self-denial is where we lose the battle so many times in temptation. We simply will not deny ourselves much of anything that appeals to the flesh. No wonder the first thing Jesus said to those who would follow Him was to "deny himself' (Matthew 16:24). The world, however, in contrast to what Christ advocates, is busy telling us we are entitled to everything. The "rights" movement is rooted and grounded in that philosophy and deplores the idea that we should go without, be denied something, or be restricted. But behind the promotion of the "rights" movement is the devil who knows that once we embrace the "rights" movement we have shoved self-denial right out the door. No man, however, will live successfully for God who does not know how to deny self. No one will successfully do battle with temptation who does not practice self-denial.

Third, he was *God-honoring*. Gideon refused the request because it was not his place to be king. "The LORD shall rule over you" was his response. "Gideon knew too well, and revered too piously, the principles of the theocracy to entertain the proposal for a moment . . . every worldly motive was kept in check by the supreme regard to the Divine honor" (Jamieson).

Temptation will lose its power with us when we insist in our conduct being God-honoring. When we insist on giving God first place, when we insist on acknowledging the Word of God as the supreme authority, and when we insist that His honor be above ours, then we will conquer temptation instead of being conquered by it. Joseph used the honor of God as one of the key weapons to defeat his great temptation from Potiphar's wife. He said to her, "How then can I do this great wickedness, and sin against God?" (Genesis 39:9). Because he wanted to honor God with his life, temptation lost its power with him. The same will be true with us, too.

B. THE DONATION REQUEST

Gideon followed the request of the people with a request of his own. After turning down their request for him to be king, he said, "I would desire a request of you, that ye would give me every man the earrings of his prey" (v. 24). Gideon wanted the people to make a donation from their war plunder. They had accumulated a number of valuables from the spoils of the war with Midian, "golden earrings . . . ornaments, and collars, and purple raiment that was on the kings of Midian . . . beside the chains that were about their camels' necks" (vv. 24, 26). Of this plunder, Gideon particularly wanted them to donate the golden earrings; so he could make an ephod and put it in Ophrah where he lived (v. 27).

We could wish that Gideon's request had never been made and that the story in our text had ended with Gideon's gallant refusal of the people's request for him to be king. But, unfortunately, the story does not end there. It continues and ingloriously. With his request, Gideon goes from a great victory to a great defeat. Back to back are grace and guile, virtue and vileness, and good and evil. In one breath, Gideon turns down a temptation; but in the next breath, he yields to a temptation. His request was no better than the people's request.

We will consider the response of the people to this request, the reason for the request, and the ruin from the request.

1. The Response to the Request

Unlike Gideon, the people did not refuse the request given them. After Gideon made his request, they said, "We will willingly give them. And they spread a garment, and did cast therein every man the earrings of his prey. And the weight of the golden earrings that he requested was a thousand and seven hundred shekels" (vv. 25, 26). Being very willing to give to Gideon, the people immediately and generously responded to Gideon's request. Their gifts totaled a considerable amount. The weight, translated into our weight, is anywhere from fifty pounds (Keil) to sixty-six pounds (Wiseman). That means a lot of gold! Gideon took up quite an offering that day.

How often it is that people will give more quickly and more liberally to a cause that is suspect than to a good and valid cause. Gideon's cause here was not valid, as we will see shortly; but the people gave generously anyway and without asking questions. Yet, when his cause was just and right, the people of Succoth and Penuel quizzed him and would not give him even a loaf of bread, let alone many pounds of gold.

We see this same practice on every hand today. The most worthless programs and causes seem to have little difficulty getting backers. But a genuine, worthy ministry is generally mistrusted, scrutinized, and begrudgingly supported even though it is impeccable and everything is on top of the table. So the sex-scandalized PTL took in millions while godly missionaries had trouble getting several thousand for their missionary support, and Schuler and his house of glass can lift a fortune from people while true churches struggle to make ends meet.

One of the main reasons that inequity in giving occurs is the poor spiritual condition of the people. Those giving to Gideon had little spiritual depth. They had already been advocating a program contrary to God's will. Therefore, it is not surprising that they donated so freely to Gideon's cause, for they had no spiritual discernment. They did not have enough spiritual wisdom to even ask Gideon why he wanted the gold. Like many, they were too taken up with the man to investigate his program. Yes, some of the TV evangelists and others who fleece the people have a lot of charisma and clever disguises to fool people. But if people had much spiritual discernment at all, they would not give to any of these programs. The success of these programs is only a testimony to the poor spiritual condition of the givers.

2. The Reason for the Request

"And Gideon made an ephod thereof, and put it in his city, even in Ophrah" (v. 27). The reason Gideon made his request for gold was so he could make an ephod. This was a very wrong thing for him to do; for the making of an ephod and putting it in Ophrah, where he lived, manifested his desire to function as Israel's High Priest, a duty and position assigned only to the descendants of Aaron. The ephod spoke unequivocally of the ministry of Israel's High Priest. In a very generic sense, an ephod is simply a sleeveless, outer vest which in length generally extended to the hips. But an ephod is not used in a generic sense in Scripture. In the Old Testament (where the ephod is exclusively mentioned in Scripture), it refers to the special garment of the High Priest except in a few rare occasions where the reference is made in such a way as to clearly distinguish it from the High Priest's garment. Thus whenever you see a reference to an ephod in the Bible, it always refers to the High Priest's garment unless clearly stated otherwise.

This garment, described in Exodus 28, was a very beautiful, elaborate, rich, and bejeweled garment. It was made of "gold, of blue, and of purple, of scarlet, and fine twined linen, with skillful work" (Exodus 28:6). It included the Urim and the Thummim which were used to discern God's will especially during times of crisis. It represented special intermediacy with God and special revelation from God—hence it represented high spiritual privilege, position, and esteem.

The High Priest wore this ephod when performing his official priestly duties; although after some years, it appears the ephod was carried and not always worn when fulfilling High Priestly duties (cp. I Samuel 23:6,9). Gideon's ephod, by what is said of it ("put it in his city"), may not have been worn either. It may have been a gold replica of the High Priest's ephod mounted in some significant place near his home in Ophrah. But whether Gideon actually made a garment (much gold was used even in the garment of the High Priest as Exodus 28 relates) or a gold replica of it, the ephod would still serve the purpose of designating special priestly position and privilege.

So the main reason behind the donation request was Gideon's desire to function as a very special spiritual leader of Israel. He wanted the authority, position, respect, and privileges of a High Priest. The ephod would give this to him, for "The ephod would be a witness that he was in a place of exclusive and peculiar nearness to God" (Ridout). This is something the flesh covets greedily, for few things are so attractive to fleshly pride as to be in an esteemed position of spiritual superiority. Flesh is not interested in true spirituality, of course, but it covets the respect and honor people give to one who has spiritual position, authority, insight, and leadership.

The fact that Israel already had a High Priest did not interfere with Gideon's plans. At that time, the Tabernacle and High Priest were in Shiloh which was located in Ephraim. But since apostasy was so strong prior to the war with Midian, true worship, which was centered in Shiloh, was much neglected and, as happened frequently in Israel during times of apostasy, would also be much corrupted. Gideon, therefore, decided he would correct the situation by having an ephod at Ophrah. After all, he could reason, he was singled out of all Israel to be visited by the Angel of the Lord, given special revelations and signs, instructed to make an altar unto God, and told to offer sacrifices which were in fact accepted by God (Judges 6). But Gideon's error was in assuming that this special and temporary spiritual privilege he had experienced constituted a permanent situation and gave him the power to oversee Israel's religious functions. He ignored the obvious interim nature of his special revelation and spiritual privileges from God. He ignored the fact that God, in granting these revelations and privileges, had not in any way forsaken the Aaronic priesthood order and given it to Gideon, anymore than God, in making Gideon Israel's deliverer from Midian, had forsaken the theocracy to make Gideon king. But the prestige of revelation and spiritual privilege would encourage him to make his experience a permanent office even though it usurped the Divinely ordained office. "Gideon resisted the temptation to put an earthly crown upon his head, from true fidelity to Jehovah; but he yielded to another temptation . . . His sin . . . consisted chiefly in his invading the prerogative of the Aaronic priesthood" (Keil). He aspired to a spiritual position which was not his.

Gideon's failure was not an unusual occurrence. Many others have failed in the same way. The fall of Satan occurred because he coveted a spiritual position that did not belong to him, being motivated by the glory that was involved in the coveted position. The temptation of Adam and Eve in the Garden of Eden embodied the same failure as Gideon's. "Ye shall be as gods" (Genesis 3:5) had a strong appeal to their fleshly pride. King Uzziah practically duplicated Gideon's failure. In his pride, he also performed the duty that only a priest was to perform (II Chronicles 26:16–19). The failure of Gideon is seen in men who enter the ministry without a Divine call because their fleshly pride covets the spiritual status and esteem that accompanies this calling. Women who get out of place in the church because they have arrogated to themselves the place of spiritual leadership, which has never been their prerogative to have, reflect Gideon's failure. From women ordained to the ministry to nothing more than women who are outspoken and vocal in a church business meeting, this spiritual presumption of women evidences itself in a very disgusting and disrupting manner. Others repeat Gideon's failure when they aspire for a church office they are unqualified for either by their moral failures or by their lack of skills to perform the office. And some imitate his failure by presumptuously assuming much more authority for their church office than what the church constitution gives it. Gideon has indeed had many follow in his footsteps of spiritual pride.

3. The Ruin From the Request

Gideon's ephod, which resulted from his request, brought much ruin to the land. "All Israel went thither a whoring after it: which thing became a snare unto Gideon, and to his house" (v. 27). The ruin was threefold. It brought ruin to an individual, it brought ruin to a family, and it brought ruin to a nation. This ruin is predictable; for when religion is corrupted, it will eventually corrupt conduct. An unholy creed is the basis for unholy conduct. Doctrine and deportment are inseparable.

It brought ruin to an individual. It "became a snare unto Gideon." F. C. Cook clarified the meaning of "snare" when he said the meaning is not "as the phrase in English rather suggests, [namely] a means of drawing them unawares into idolatry; but [it means] a cause of ruin." With the ephod, Gideon got to play the part he wanted to play, for "all Israel went there [to his dwelling]" because of it. But what a price he paid for gaining position and esteem in spiritual things which did not rightfully belong to him. He ruined himself. As we will see in our next chapter, part of the ruin was incurred through a low moral lifestyle.

He who leads others astray spiritually will be ruined himself. The morally rotten religious leaders who have in recent years been exposed for their wretched lifestyles, are simply additional illustrations of what happened in Gideon's life when he led his people astray spiritually. One cannot mislead people spiritually without being destroyed in the process.

It brought ruin to a family. The ephod not only became a snare to Gideon, but it also was a "snare . . . to his house." Great ruin came to Gideon's family shortly after he died. His son from a concubine rose up and slew all but one of Gideon's seventy sons in an attempt to gain the rule over the land (Judges 8:31; 9:1–6). Such conduct had its roots in a corrupted religion which had brought corruption in morals.

A corrupt religion does not help the family. It does not promote the home; it destroys the home. One wonders about the real creed of some of our fundamental churches who claim to be sound theologically, but whose position and attitude regarding the moral problem of divorce only encourages and sanctions the breakup of homes.

It brought ruin to a nation. "All Israel went thither a whoring after it." A corrupt religion will bring much ruin in a nation. It may have big crowds and much appeal, but it is a menace to any nation. Gideon had delivered Israel from the oppression of Midian, but he did not deliver them from the root of their problems. When he died they went right back to Baal worship

(Judges 8:33); for when you corrupt true religion, you lay the foundation for people to embrace false religion. This then resulted in Israel again coming under the oppression of an enemy.

What a tragedy occurred because of this request by Gideon. It was Gideon's great fall. He, who had delivered himself, his family, and his nation from great oppression and ruin, paved the way for future oppression and ruin by this request. Gideon's request used the spoils of one victory over oppression to bring on another oppression. Though he guided Israel to a tremendous victory over Midian and in so doing demonstrated great faith, yet he failed in the end because of spiritual pride. It is a very solemn and sobering warning to all.

XI.

Relapse

Judges 8:28–35

GIDEON'S GREAT WORK of delivering Israel from the Midianite oppression brought great benefits to Israel. The benefits are summed up in the last sentence of verse 28: "And the country was in quietness forty years in the days of Gideon." The word "quietness," according to Wilson (*Old Testament Word Studies*), describes one "who is never infested [bothered by great numbers or frequency of trials], harassed, troubled; and of one who has no fear or dread." So there was great peace and security in the land of Israel. The people could go about their business of living their lives without fear of enemy nations invading, plundering, and killing.

But that quietness was misused. It was not used to build up the faith and strengthen the soul. Rather, as is often the case, the newly obtained freedom and security were used to pamper the desires of the flesh. Leisure was made an opportunity for lusting. Prosperity promoted sinfulness, not righteousness. Therefore, instead of progressing spiritually after their initial revival just prior to the deliverance from Midian, Gideon and Israel walked in the path of continual moral and spiritual decline. There was a general relapse in both Gideon's conduct and that of his fellow countrymen.

This relapse certainly does not provide a very good ending to the story of Gideon, a story which had commenced so promising with a series of glorious performances because of faith in God. But the faithfulness of the Scripture to record the truth of our heroes is a great testimony of the veracity of the

Word of God. If man were writing this story of Gideon, he would not report the inglorious end. He would probably stop the story after Gideon turned down the offer to be Israel's king. That would have provided a great ending for the story of Gideon. But the Word of God does not whitewash. It records the bad as well as the good. Thus it records Moses' weakness as well as his greatness; it records David's sins as well as his successes; it records Elijah's lapse of faith as well as his largeness of faith; it records the faults as well as the faith of Peter and Paul; and it records Gideon's vileness as well as his victory. Yes, God records both the negative and the positive of our heroes, and He does it for our needed instruction. "Their virtues are described so that we may imitate them, their vices depicted that we may avoid them" (William Burrows).

This faithful recording of both the good and the bad reminds us that God is recording everything about us, too. If we were to write our own life, we would doubtless follow the habits of all those who write their own biographies. We would emphasize the good and ignore or minimize or favorably interpret the bad. It would not be a true story. But God only writes truth, and when He writes our story it will record all about us, including all our sins; not one sin will be ignored. Therefore, if we are wise, we will confess our sins (instead of denying, minimizing, or excusing them) to Jesus Christ and plead for His blood to wash them away. Apart from this, we have no hope of escaping eternal condemnation when we stand before God in judgment; for He knows about all our sins, and He will judge accordingly unless we have had our sins washed away by the blood of Christ.

In this final chapter on Gideon, we will consider the conqueror's relapse and the country's relapse. They are inseparably related. The relapse of Gideon only encouraged his people to do the same.

A. THE CONQUEROR'S RELAPSE

"And Jerubbaal [Gideon] . . . went and dwelt in his own house [and] . . . died in a good old age, and was buried in the sepulcher of Joash, his father, in Ophrah of the Abiezrites" (vv. 29, 32). After defeating the Midianites, Gideon went back to his home in Ophrah to live out the rest of his life. He enjoyed longevity ("died in a good old age") and had an honorable burial ("buried in the sepulcher of Joash, his father"). But he did not live a noble life.

Some have a tendency to gloss over Gideon's shameful relapse because he is said to have died "in a good old age" and had an honorable burial. But longevity and an honorable burial do not necessarily indicate a noble life, for a number of very wicked men have lived many years, and many of these wicked men have had very elaborate funerals, too. So it was with Gideon. Between verse 29, which records Gideon's return to his home, and verse 32, which records his longevity and honorable death, is recorded some very unholy living by Gideon. Though Gideon had performed superbly in fighting the Midianites, his great work of delivering Israel from the Midianite oppression was not followed by worthy deeds. Instead of continuing the pursuit of a higher way of life, which he had begun after the initial visit of the angel of the Lord to him, he went back to living like the world. It is a very disappointing relapse for the reader to behold. It is also a very defiled lifestyle to behold. So much so that William Burrows, who described Gideon's refusal of the crown as "Gideon at his best," fittingly describes these last few verses on Gideon as "Gideon at his worst."

Our text records two particular ways in which this relapse of Gideon is most evident. These two ways are the size of his family and the source of his family.

1. The Size of His Family
"And Gideon had threescore and ten sons of his body begotten: for he had many wives" (v. 30). It is not evil per se to have seventy sons, for you could adopt a number of sons. But having seventy sons from one's own "body begotten" is not possible if one is going to live on a high moral plane regarding marriage, for to have seventy sons of your own flesh will require a number

of women. To have seventy sons, Gideon practiced gross polygamy; for he had "many wives."

Having a multiplicity of wives is a very morally degrading practice. Yes, we see a lot of it in the Old Testament, and even some of the revered patriarchs practiced it. But that certainly does not sanction it. In fact, where we see it practiced, we always see serious problems from it—and such serious problems that even if God did not specifically forbid it, we still would not be encouraged to practice it because of the problems associated with it. God gave Adam one wife. That was the way it was always intended to be. But it did not take long before man in his lustfulness began multiplying his wives. Significantly, it was the unholy line of Cain which is first recorded as having a plurality of wives. Lamech, the fifth in line from Cain, "took unto him two wives" (Genesis 4:19).

In having many wives, Gideon not only violated a Divine principle about marriage, but he also ignored the teaching of Scripture about Israel's leaders having more than one wife. Scripture was plain in forbidding a leader to practice polygamy. "Neither shall he multiply wives to himself" (Deuteronomy 17:17). This law was especially written for Israel's future kings, for the common practice of the day was for kings to have many wives so they could have many sons. It was considered the politically expedient thing for the leader of a country to have many sons. This was supposed to strengthen his political power and his rule and enhance the longevity of his dynasty. Gideon was not a king; but he was still Israel's leader, specifically their judge; and so his position would come under the philosophy of the day, namely, have many sons to strengthen your rule. Hence, he practiced what was common among the rulers of nations in those days.

This practice would certainly appeal to the flesh, for it would appeal to Gideon's sensual desires (many wives) and to his pride (seventy sons). But the idea that this practice would strengthen a leader's situation was a bold lie from the pit of hell. This kind of morality never strengthened any government or any family; rather, it always weakened the rule and the family involved. This certainly was the case with Gideon. Shortly after he died, his family was nearly wiped out by the murderous action of an offspring of his unrestrained sensual activity (Judges 9:5), and his family soon ceased to rule in Israel.

Today, we still practice the multiplicity of wives. However, we do not do it for the same purpose as men did in Old Testament times; for we do not do it to strengthen our political powers, etc. We do it solely because of lust. Neither do we practice polygamy to have a multiplicity of wives, for we only have one wife at a time. To have a number of wives we simply practice divorce. When we get tired of one wife, we divorce that wife and marry another. But morally there is no difference between this and polygamy. Divorce is nothing but lustful behavior that degrades all who are involved. It produces many great problems for society, too, just as polygamy did in Old Testament times. But, in spite of the degradation of the practice and in spite of the problems divorce causes, our laws make all this multiplicity of wives as legitimate as possible.

When it comes to the Scripture, however, the conclusion that this method of having a multiplicity of wives is legitimate will not fly. Scripture clearly teaches that a man is to have but one wife unless she dies; then and then only can he marry another woman. But that is not popular today, even among conservative fundamental Christians. This lack of popularity among professing Christians is why we have so many flesh-appealing, perverted interpretations of Bible texts which speak on this subject. It is also why folk are forever looking for loophole texts in Scripture to sanction their divorce actions. Furthermore, it is why preachers are so busy sanctioning divorce and remarriage, rather than thundering out against it. These preachers want to gain a crowd; and today if you want to appeal to the crowd, you had better not come down very hard on divorce; for it is almost impossible to get a crowd in your church if you take an adamant stand against divorce and remarriage.

2. The Source of His Family

"And his concubine, that was in Shechem, she also bare him a son, whose name he called Abimelech" (v. 31). Gideon did not limit himself to having children just from wives. He also had a concubine. This morally-degrading, woman-enslaving practice was bad enough in itself, but what made it worse in Gideon's case was that the concubine was a Canaanite from Shechem. Israel had no business flirting with Canaanitish women. Furthermore, Shechem was a warning to Israel about what happens when God's people fraternize too closely with the Canaanites; for Dinah, Jacob's daughter, was morally defiled by one of the men of Shechem. Shechem was a moral dung hill, and Gideon got too close to it.

The product of this vile venture of Gideon was a son named Abimelech. That such an offspring should be a benefit to a government or family, as was thought in those days, is quickly shot down by the record of Judges chapter 9, which we referred to briefly a bit earlier. That chapter records how Abimelech, upon Gideon's death, aspired to reign over the people; and in order to gain this power, he slaughtered all but one of Gideon's other seventy sons. Then, after he had reigned a few years, he in turn was slain when a mill stone was dropped on his head from the top of a tower which he and his troops were besieging. His whole rule was weak, unproductive, and divisive; and he died as he had lived. It is a shameful story which came about because of unholy morals.

Concubines were common in the Old Testament, so common that even some of the great patriarchs and leaders of Israel had concubines. But that does not sanction them in the slightest anymore than polygamy was sanctioned by the fact that some of Israel's great patriarchs and leaders practiced it. Yet, how often we excuse people from wrong doing if an evil practice they pursue happens to be common in society. Satan loves to make wicked practices so common that they are simply accepted as the norm. But we must not accept some form of conduct just because it is nearly universal in practice. We have a better, more trustworthy, more noble standard than that! We have the Word of God. Therefore, regardless of how common something is, we need to examine it in the light of the Word of God. If the Word condemns it, we must also condemn it and not practice it.

B. THE COUNTRY'S RELAPSE

The very evident relapse of the country was, as we noted earlier, related to Gideon's relapse; and it followed on the heels of Gideon's death. While some indications of the relapse were discernible before his death, it was his death which triggered Israel's wholesale reverting to their evil ways. The relapse of Israel was especially manifested in their idolatry and their ingratitude.

1. The Idolatry of Israel

"And it came to pass, as soon as Gideon was dead, that the children of Israel turned again, and went a whoring after Baalim, and made Baal-berith their god" (v. 33). It was the back to Baal movement for Israel. Gideon had led Israel away from Baal in the early days of his leadership. This spiritual reformation began when he tore down the altar of Baal which belonged to his father and which served as a place for Baal worship for his community. This courageous act, which inspired others to stop worshipping Baal, resulted in Gideon being called Jerubbaal, which signifies he was a Baal-fighter.

However, the fact that the relapse of Israel into idolatry was connected so closely to Gideon's death indicated a lack of genuineness in Israel's professed reformation. While Gideon was alive, they appeared to be following Jehovah; but "as soon as Gideon was dead" their true heart was revealed. They were only held back from Baal worship by the influence of Gideon, not by a heart given in devotion to Jehovah. Therefore, their faith was not true faith; for it was not grounded on the Word of God. It was a faith which was built on a man, namely, Gideon. When he died, their faith died.

Many in our churches are like that. Such members appear to

be fundamental, Bible-believing, and true Christians. But take away their spiritual hero or their favorite preacher, and their faith disappears; for their faith is not founded on the Word of God but on some personality. Being founded on a personality rather than the Word makes these professing, but not possessing, Christians vulnerable to being easily and quickly led astray. They can be easily led astray by the man they so ardently follow, and they can be easily led astray by others after their hero passes from the scene. Let us look at these two perils in more detail.

First, they can be easily led astray by the man they so ardently follow. There can be much deviating from the Word of God in worship, in doctrine, and in conduct by their leader; but they will continue to follow him anyway because he, not the Word of God, is their guide. Hence, the Israelites in Gideon's time did not object to the ephod Gideon wrongly injected into their worship of Jehovah. They were following a man and not the Word, so "all Israel went thither a whoring after it" (Judges 8:27). Today we have some famous men in our fundamental churches who in their practice have deviated a great deal from the Word of God. But their followers continue to attend the churches pastored by these famous men, for the followers' faith is not based primarily on what the Word says but on what their hero says.

Second, they can be easily led astray by others after their hero passes from the scene. When Gideon died, his followers were easily and quickly persuaded to go back to Baal. Since their faith was in Gideon, and not in the eternal, unchanging Word of God, they had no faith left to anchor their soul and keep themselves from error when Gideon died. In our times, this happened very notably in the case of Joseph Parker and T. DeWitt Talmadge. When Parker died, his followers in City Temple in London fell into the hands of R. J. Campbell, founder of the New Theology. When Talmadge died, the Brooklyn Tabernacle fell into the hands of Charles T. Russell and the Jehovah Witnesses' group. While Parker and Talmadge preached the truth, too many of their listeners were simply followers of them and not of the Word they preached. But our faith must be in the Word, not in man, if it is to be real and stand the tests of life.

2. The Ingratitude of Israel

"And the children of Israel remembered not the LORD their God, who had delivered them out of the hands of all their enemies on every side: Neither showed they kindness to the house of Jerubbaal, namely, Gideon, according to all the goodness which he had shown unto Israel" (vv. 34, 35).

Israel's ingratitude was twofold. They manifested ingratitude to God and to Gideon.

Ingratitude to God. Israel manifested their ingratitude to God by forgetting Him. Though God had worked so miraculously for them in delivering them from their enemies, the Midianites, Israel forgot God and went after Baal. And they did this even though it was Baal worship that had brought them all the trouble with the Midianites earlier. How stupid ingratitude makes us.

This is not the first time Israel has shown their ingratitude by forgetting God. Psalm 78 records some other times when this problem plagued them. After God delivered them from Egypt and other enemies, the testimony of Israel was that they "forgat his works, and his wonders that he had showed them" (v. 11), and "They remembered not his hand, nor the day when he delivered them from the enemy" (v. 42).

Israel's interest in God was too often self-serving. When they were in trouble they sought God, but when prosperity came they forgot Him. "Selfishness inclines us to remember God only when we want his aid" (W. F. Adeney). This certainly mirrors the way our nation behaves. When our nation comes to a time of distress, the President often calls upon the people to pray, encourages special prayer services in churches and other places, counsels with various ministers, and shows up conspicuously in church himself for special services of prayer. But when the crisis is over, it is business as usual. That means it is business without God. Little time or mention is given to thanking God for His great help in the crisis, God's ways are violated unashamedly, and the courts continue to exclude God from schools and public places. We, like Israel of old, remember not the Lord our God.

Such a practice is fraught with great peril, of course. It brought upon Israel, as it will bring upon any nation, great troubles. However, if we want real and lasting quietness in the land, then we must learn not only to pursue God in our troubles, but also to praise God in our triumphs just as earnestly as we pursued Him in our troubles.

Ingratitude to Gideon. Israel demonstrated their ingratitude for Gideon by failing to show kindness to Gideon's family. When we have the problem of verse 34 (ingratitude to God), we will also have the problem of verse 35 (ingratitude to Gideon). "Ingratitude to God is joined to ingratitude to his servants" (W. F. Adeney).

Israel's appreciation for Gideon's valor declined as the years went by. They relapsed back to their behavior prior to the Midianite war when they were ready to kill Gideon when he had torn down the altar of Baal. So after Gideon had died, the attitude in the land became so unappreciative for Gideon that nearly all of Gideon's sons could be slaughtered without protection from society (Judges 9:1–5). Gideon had saved many of Israel's sons from death by the victory over Midian, but Israel did not reciprocate. Jotham, the only son who escaped the murderous action of Abimelech and his followers, admonished the murderers regarding this ingratitude when he said, "For my father fought for you, and adventured [risked] his life far, and delivered you out of the hand of Midian: And ye are risen up against my father's house this day, and have slain his sons, threescore and ten persons, upon one stone, and have made Abimelech, the son of his maidservant, king over the men of Shechem, because he is your brother; If ye then have dealt truly and sincerely with

Relapse

Jerubbaal and with his house this day, then rejoice ye in Abimelech, and let him also rejoice in you: But if not, let fire come out from Abimelech, and devour the men of Shechem, and the house of Millo; and let fire come out from the men of Shechem, and from the house of Millo, and devour Abimelech" (Judges 9:17–20). Our conduct towards men reflects our conduct towards God. The better we treat God, the better we will treat man. "We are not likely to be true to man until we are first true to God" (W. F. Adeney). "Those who forget their God forget their friends" (Matthew Henry). Jesus emphasized this truth when He said the first and great commandment was "Thou shalt love the Lord thy God with all thy heart, and with all thy soul, and with all thy mind" (Matthew 22:37); and that the second commandment was, "Thou shalt love thy neighbor as thyself" (Matthew 22:39). As Joseph Parker said, "There is logic in the sequence of the commandments." It all begins with God. If we cannot love God right, we will not love man right. Israel forgot the work God did for them, so we should not be surprised that they forgot what Gideon had done for them. "The heart of stone which is not touched by the love of Christ is also insensible to the kindness of man" (A. C. Hervey).

So our study of Gideon ends with ungrateful Israel failing to show kindness to Gideon's family even though Gideon had done so much for the Israelites. But this is ever the history of man, especially in regards to the greatest deliverer of all, Jesus Christ. No one has done more for mankind than Jesus Christ. He has gone to the cross to conquer the great Midianite tyrant of our soul and thus provide for us the great "quietness" (v. 28) that peace with God produces. Yet, men fail to show their gratitude to Christ for His tremendous work by failing to show kindness to His people. Therefore, Christians all around the world are persecuted, hunted down, imprisoned, and martyred by these ungrateful people. But, as in Jotham's admonition, fire will devour these ingrates. The fire of hell will judge all those who have such ingratitude in their hearts for Jesus Christ.

Quotation Sources

The person listed is the author of the book which follows his name unless an asterisk (*) appears after the book title. In this case the person is a contributor to the book or is quoted in the book. Our quoting a person does not mean we necessarily endorse all the beliefs, practices, or associations of that person.

Adeney, W. F. *The Pulpit Commentary (Vol. 3).**
Baxter, J. Sidlow. *Explore the Book (Vol. 1).*
Bevan, H. E. J. *The Biblical Illustrator (Vol. 3).**
Burrows, William. *The Biblical Illustrator (Vol. 3).**
Cambron, Mark. *Bible Doctrines.*
Cook, F. C. *The Bible Commentary (Vol. 1).*
DeHaan, M. R. *Broken Things.*
Dods, Marcus. *The Biblical Illustrator (Vol. 3).**
Duncan, W. W. *The Biblical Illustrator (Vol. 3).**
Edersheim, Alfred. *The Bible History, Old Testament.*
Edwards, Henry T. *The Biblical Illustrator (Vol. 3).**
Elwin, F. *The Biblical Illustrator (Vol. 3).**
Haldeman, I. M. *Bible Expositions (Vol. 1).*
Hamly, J. T. *The Biblical Illustrator (Vol. 3).**
Henry, Matthew. *Commentary on the Whole Bible (Vol. 2).*
Hervey, A. C. *The Pulpit Commentary (Vol. 3).**
Jamieson, Robert. *A Commentary (Vol. 1).*
Jones, J. D. *The Biblical Illustrator (Vol. 3)**
Keil, C. F. *Commentary on the Old Testament (Vol. 2).*
Kelly, T. *The Biblical Illustrator (Vol. 3).**
Maclaren, Alexander. *Expositions of the Holy Scripture (Vol. 1).*
Mason, Edward B. *The Biblical Illustrator (Vol. 3).**
Meyer, F. B. *Choice Notes on Joshua to II Kings.*
Miller W. *The Biblical Illustrator (Vol. 3).**
Muir A. F. *The Pulpit Commentary (Vol. 3).**
Parker, Joseph. *Preaching Through the Bible (Vol. 3).*
Poole, Matthew. *A Commentary on the Holy Bible (Vol. 1).*
Ridout, Samuel. *Judges and Ruth.*
Rogers, G. A. *The Biblical Illustrator (Vol. 3).**

Simeon, Charles. *Expository Outlines on the Whole Bible (Vol. 3).*
Smith, James. *Handfuls on Purpose (Vol. 4).*
Watson, R. A. *The Biblical Illustrator (Vol. 3).**
Wilson, William. *Old Testament Word Studies.*
Wiseman, Luke H. *Practical Truths from Judges.*